Edwin MacMinn

A German Hero of the Colonial Times of Pennsylvania

The Life and Times of Henry Antes

Edwin MacMinn

A German Hero of the Colonial Times of Pennsylvania
The Life and Times of Henry Antes

ISBN/EAN: 9783337155193

Printed in Europe, USA, Canada, Australia, Japan

Cover: Foto ©ninafisch / pixelio.de

More available books at **www.hansebooks.com**

—OF THE—

COLONIAL TIMES OF PENNSYLVANIA;

—OR THE—

LIFE AND TIMES OF HENRY ANTES,

—BY—

REV. EDWIN MCMINN.

Dedication.

To my mother, the daughter of Amelia Antes, this life of her ancestor is affectionately dedicated with the spirit of gratitude that in the succeeding generations a love for the work of the Lord Jesus Christ and zeal for christian union upon the bases of God's word has been effective in continuing in active service the spirit and love of their ancestor.

PREFACE.

We naturally feel proud of the elegance, wealth, and commercial importance of our beautiful Philadelphia, and take sweet delight in the fertility and beauty of the surrounding country. We see it in its strength and development, and to many it seems that it never could have been otherwise.

But Clio comes to warn us from such a conclusion, and points to us the weather stained, mouldy and faded fragments of the days gone by, and out of these we learn what perils, trials and sufferings, what poverty and need, beset our forefathers as they laid the foundations of the prosperity which we now enjoy.

In this volume we may see what life was in Philadelphia and the surrounding country a hundred and fifty years ago.

To the writer, this period is exceedingly attractive, the more so because his ancestor, Henry Antes, was one of the leading spirits of that time, and in the story of his life the spirit of his time can be plainly discerned.

In the preparation of this historical information, I am indebted to Mr. Henry S. Dotterer, more than to all others, for having thoroughly searched the records and gleaned the facts as to the work of Henry Antes, and only his cordial encouragement, and generosity in placing at my disposal his information, could have induced me to persevere in the preparation of this volume.

Mr. John W. Jordan, also kindly looked over the MSS. and gave me correct information on several points of doubt.

My thanks are also due to the distinguished scholars, Prof. Oscar Seidensticker and S. W. Pennypacker, for information which they have gleaned from ancient records. At this present day no one can write the early history of our State and particularly of the German settlers without being greatly indebted to them for the thoroughness and carefulness of their investigations.

I am also greatly indebted to Major L. H. Evarts for so kindly permitting me to use as fully as I might desire for my purpose the History of Philadelphia, and the History of Montgomery County, with illustrations, as published by him.

To my uncle, George W. Youngman, I am indebted for first of all calling my attention to the historical importance of Henry Antes, and to financial assistance in publishing this volume.

To my brother, H. S. McMinn, I am indebted for a list of the descendants, which after years of searching he had succeeded in properly classifying.

And to the many subscribers who have shown their interest in such a work by encouraging its publication I now return my sincere thanks, and hope that they will not be disappointed in the volume now placed before them. There is a possibility that some future day we may undertake a similar work on the life of Henry Antes' three distinguished sons.

TABLE OF CONTENTS.

Chapter 1. **The Religious Wars in the Palatinate**, and the fall of the house of Von Blume,   11

" 2. **The founding of Pennsylvania by William Penn**, and his invitation to the Germans. Penn's arrival on the ship Welcome, with his company of Quaker settlers; wintering in the Province,   19

" 3. **The Germans.** The Mennonites purchase 25,000 acres of land. Coming of Francis Daniel Pastorius; his scholarship. Emigrants from Crefeld. Founding of Germantown. Their simplicity, style of living; weavers and mill builders. Protest against slavery. Town laws. William Dewees. Attempt to restrict German emigration. Printing the Bible,   30

" 4. **The Indians.**—Their numbers, appearance, language, customs, marriage, houses, liberality, love of strong drink, religion, government, bargaining, tools, tattooing, dress, money, wampum, value of a piece of land, Indian tracks, wigwams,   41

5. **Emigration and Settlement in the Wilderness.** The Frankfort Company's tract. Coming of Emigrants without records of their names and dates. Henry Antes. Perils of the voyage. The land they left contrasted with the wilderness. The meadows. William Dewees' paper mill on the Wissahickon. Henry Antes' abilities. Settlers' houses. Furniture. Stalwart manhood and social songs in the forest,   55

" 6. **The Hermits in the Wilderness.** Dr. Witt. Henry Antes' courtship. Boehm assumes ministerial offices. The marriage festivities of Henry Antes,   65

Chapter 7. Scenes on the Wissahickon. The Crefeld mill. Indian burden bearers. The Tunkers from the wilderness. The classes of settlers, 75

" 8. Philadelphia in 1730. Danger from Indians. Act of Naturalization. Franklin's Gazette. Philadelphia Library established. The building of the State House. London coffee House. The Quakers. George Washington born. The frontier physician, 83

" 9. Religious Colonists. The Unitas Fratrum. The history and doctrines. The Schwenkfelders. Moravian settlers in Georgia. Cottage prayer meetings. Antes builds his house and the first grist mill is erected in the wilderness, 95

" 10. Contemporary Events. The small pox plague. Great ice flood. Visit by John Penn. The Conestoga hermit. Indian council. Trouble on the border. Land claims, 104

" 11. Spangenberg and Whitefield. Birth of John Henry Antes. The Associated Brethren of Skippack. Death in the household. Christian Union. Birth of John Antes. Andrew Eschenback. Whitefield's surprising eloquence. Nazareth started, 109

" 12. The Founding of Bethlehem. Colonial quarrels and distress. War threatened. Restrictions on commerce. The plague in the city. The Germans flattered. The Lazaretto. Riots at elections. Antes' religious work in the country. Lutheran view of the state of religion. Reformed view. Strong denominationalism. Bethlehem selected, 122

" 13. Unity Conferences. Count Zinzendorf. The call for the conferences. The work of the conference. Antes' letter to the people of Pennsylvania. Boehm's letter against Antes, 134

" 14. Indian Tribes on the Border. Antes' mission. The council of the Indians and the Governor's treatment of them. The Six Nations condemning the Delawares. Arrival of a colony of Moravians. Busy days. New acts for naturalization. Zinzendorf's return to Europe. Departure of Antes' daughter. Printing the German Bible, 152

Chapter 15. **Moravian Schools and Education.** Philadelphia in 1744. War between France and Great Britain. Franklin's efforts. Military lottery. Antes gives his home. The colonial Justice. Canoe warfare on the Schuylkill, 164.

" 16. **Antes' Labor for the Moravians.** Whitefield's visit with Antes. The sore throat epidemic. Privateersmen on the seas. Antes defends the Moravians at Newtown. Builds mill at Gnadenthal. The first ferry across the Lehigh. Visit to New York to launch a Moravian vessel. Appointed Consenior Civilis. The great book published at Ephrata, 172

" 17. **Separation from the Moravians. Pioneer Perils in North Carolina.** Antes protests against the white surplice. Returns to Frederick. Trip to North Carolina. Indians, fever, starvation, snow storms, perils. Rescuers and success. Antes' last work for the Moravians, 180

" 18. **The London School Movement.** The Provincial Fair. Muhlenberg's methods in training the people. This educational movement killed by newspaper influence. Antes' last defence of the Germans, 190

" 19. **Death and Burial of Antes.** Eulogies. Poetry of J. H. Dubbs. Will. Inventory, 201

" 20. **Henry M. Muhlenberg,** or the experience of this famous minister in beginning his ministry in Pennsylvania, 217

" 21. **Gottlieb Mittleberger's Book.** A description of a visit to Pennsylvania in 1750. Bringing the first organ to the Province. Fared well in the Province. Newlanders or man stealers. Six months on the journey. Delays and exposures. Horrors on the ocean. Storm at Sea. Burial. Homesickness. Hunger and thirst. First sight of land. Sold into service in Philadelphia to pay passage money. Clearing new land. Sad case of a Wurtemberger. Extent of emigration. Methods of the man stealers. Philadelphia in 1754. Religious freedom in Pennsylvania. Freedom of trades. Smartness of the young people. Going to church on horseback. Funerals. State of the churches. Pay of the clergy. Beverages. No beggars. Rural life. Trees; flowers, etc. Sunsets. Birds, etc. Snakes. Fireflies. The Indians. Remarkable discovery. Stolen marriage. Hospitality. English ladies. Mines, etc. Slaves. Earliest times. A bear story. May Fair. Old time good will. Music. Ladies' fashions in 1754. Gentlemen's apparel. Dwelling houses. Change in calendar. Highways. Return to Europe, 234

" 22. The Descendants of Henry Antes, 28:

Chapter I.

The Religious War in the Palatinate and the fall of the House of Von Blume.

OUT of great tribulations have risen characters in which the nobler qualities of mind have become crystalized, so as to exhibit their excellence in clearness and strength. Centuries of oppression have decided the fate of nations and communities. Where the character was weak, there was a gradual disappearance, but where the character was strong, there was a resistance put forth which produced a power of endurance that out of temporary defeat arose permanently triumphant.

Thus the doctrine of the survival of the fittest finds illustration.

In Germany this principle held good, and the Reformation, with the religious wars that followed, though devastating the land, have moulded a people who to-day are unsurpassed for bravery, philosophy, and religious devotion. While persecution has driven out of that land thousands who loved freedom more than life, in other lands they have founded families in which the succeeding generations have displayed the qualities which so strongly marked their ancestors, qualities which enable the descendants to stand abreast of their times, and secure to themselves honors and prosperity. When we look back to Germany we see the tremendous throes of agony through which nations must pass in their development in which all the forces of evil conspire to crush out all that is good.

Over Germany the power of Rome had extended, until the true religion of Christ was held only by refugees and mountaineers, or by a few brave souls who died for their faith in the cities where their devotion awakened a yearning among the silent thousands who observed them and believed in them as the possessors of the true gospel of the Son of God. In Bohemia John Huss fearlessly gave his testimony and died a martyr to his faith. A century after, Luther, Zwinglius, and Calvin, with their great and learned followers broke the shackles which bound the people, and Germany was taken out of the grasp of Rome, to think and worship as the hearts of the people might desire. Again a century passed and the contest spread from the university to the camp. Politics and religion were united and the most dreadful of warring convulsions shook and devastated the land. Out of this protracted season of war, through the victory of Gustavus Adolphus and the results following, came the regeneration of Germany and a religious liberty which can never again be overthrown.

Germany before the thirty years' war was vastly

different from the Germany which followed it, as we will see in a resume of the events of that period.

Among the nobility of Germany previous to that awful struggle was the baronial house of Von Blume, whose history is the same as that of hundreds of the barons involved in the storms which swept their baronies with devastation, their castles with the sword, and their families with outlawry and death, but where the personal history of a fallen house has perished, we can reconstruct it in the general history of their times. To understand therefore the fall of the house of Von Blume we must consider the history of that period, for this much is known, and it casts a beam of light athwart the history, revealing to us of the general story that which most particularly affects this individual family.

Henry, Baron Von Blume, at an early age entered the monastic life, and became an Ecclesiastic, and thus occupied a double relationship toward the state and toward Rome.

He became attached to his cousin, a Baroness, who at the time was a superior in a convent at Mayence. They became Protestants, they were married, they were victims in the awful convulsions of 1620, and amongst the proscribed hid themselves, changed their name from the German to the corresponding Greek, and a century later Henry Antes, the subject of our story, their descendant, passed out of Germany over the ocean to the Province of

Pennsylvania, to enjoy the faith for which his noble ancestor had given up nobility, castle, and fortune. To comprehend the necessity for this complete destruction of a baronial estate we refer to the history of that terrible epoch. In 1530 the Protestant princes of Germany, with the Saxon Elector at their head, had met at Smalcalde in upper Saxony, and formed a league for the defence of their liberties. For fourteen years following, there was very little interference with the religious liberties of the Germans, but in 1545 the Emperor Charles V. prepared to restore Catholicism in Germany by force of arms. The consequence was a war for seven years in southwestern Germany and in Saxony.

The result of this war was that the Protestants should enjoy the free exercise of their religion, and the Catholics should be unmolested, and that Protestants as well as Catholics should be admitted to the Imperial Chamber. This treaty was called the Peace of Religion and was solemnly confirmed at Augsberg in 1555.

The next war was for the succession of Cleves, for which numerous claimants arose. The question of this succession derived its chief importance from the circumstance that, though Protestantism had spread around them, the Dukes of Cleve had always remained attached to the orthodox church, thus constituting one of the few large Catholic powers among the temporal princes of Germany.

In the contest for the succession Wolfgang, in order to maintain himself and to gain possession of the entire Cleve inheritance solicited the Emperor to call the Spaniards into Germany. When this was done the Dutch were called in by the other parties to the claim, until a German territory, disputed by German princes, was occupied by the Spaniards for one party, and by the Dutch for the other.

This dispute continued from 1609 to 1627. The next move in the war was by the Bohemians renouncing their allegiance to Ferdinand II., and conferring the crown of Bohemia on Frederick V., elector palatine, the leading Protestant prince in Germany. This war lasted nearly six years, from 1618 to 1623 in western Germany, and is the war in which the house of Von Blume went down.

At this time there were three parties in Germany, the Catholics, the Lutherans, and the Calvinists, each party hating the other with bitter hatred, and ready to take up arms against each other on the most trifling pretexts.

And this spirit was continued until the whole of Germany was in a blaze, and death and desolation prevailed everywhere.

The Protestant union was opposed by the Catholic league, each party trying to outdo the other in avariciousness and ferocity, and whichever party held the power, the effect on the country was the same. Frederick, the Protestant leader, was very weak, and altogether incapable of managing the interests in his hands, while Ferdinand II., the Emperor, was skillful and able, and had sworn the destruction of Protestantism. Maximilian, the King of Bavaria, was also an ardent Catholic and an able general, and he too was determined on the destruction of the Protestants, and in this state of affairs the Lutherans withheld their assistance from the Calvinists, who thus left alone could not save themselves, but were defeated on every hand. Before the walls of Prague Frederick's army was cut in pieces and he became a fugitive, and then followed the Imperial edict that placed his possessions under a ban, and the Palatinate was given to the King of Bavaria. Thus Catholicism triumphed. While the Imperial and Bavarian allies were overrunning Bohemia, the Spanish general Spinola led his army of Spaniards out of the Netherlands into the Lower Palatinate where they captured place after place, and with the keenest scent for heresy hunted out those who were of the Calvinistic faith. It is at once evident that in such a search, the Baron Von Blume, a noble and ecclesiastic who had renounced Catholicism for Calvinism, would not have one stone left upon another of his castle, but would become the victim of their deepest vengeance, and this feeling would be intensified because, when the Protestants had the power, they vigorously drove out of their possessions the Catholic ecclesiastics and appropriated their benefices.

One of the followers of Frederick V. was Count Mansfield, a soldier of fortune. After the defeat of his Prince, he eluded the victorious armies of his foes and came into the Lower Palatinate with his army of twenty thousand men. He had no way of paying his soldiers except by what they could capture from their foes, and yet he held together this large force, which swarmed upon whatever rich possessions were before them. He was joined by another soldier of fortune, Duke Christian of Brunswick, with a similar army of banditti, and these were opposed by the Bavarian general Lilly, with an army which they could not successfully resist, and when hard pressed, they fled across the border and preyed upon the territories of France. The war was increased at this time by the revolt of the Huguenots in France, the Puritans were being persecuted in England, and all Europe was involved in strife. The ambition of the House of Hapsburg in Austria led them to aspire to universal control, and Richelieu in France was preparing to lay the foundations for his greatness, while Gustavus Adolphus was conquering in Poland, and making ready for the crowning work of his life, to lead and save the Protestant cause in Germany, yes, in Europe. During these years of war, the cruelties inflicted upon the defenseless people is indescribable. The population of Germany diminished in these thirty years from twenty to fifty per cent. The population of Augsburg was reduced from 80,000 to 18,000, of Wurtemburg from 400,000 to 48,000; cities, villages, castles and houses innumerable had been burned to the ground. The bare statistics of the destruction of life and property are appalling. And when at last peace spread her wings over the land, by the fortunes of war new owners possessed the land, and the former owners, knowing better than to trust the mercy or the pledge of the Catholic powers, chose to remain in obscurity, and as the way might open before them, seek protection and support for themselves, their wives, and their little ones.

If they could not bequeath to their children riches and titles of nobility, they could give them *good blood*, characters that had within them all of the elements of greatness and success, for these Catholic vengeance could not take from them, nor could obscurity hide. This was the legacy which Henry Antes received, and in turn gave to his children.

Chapter II.

The founding of Pennsylvania by William Penn, and his invitation of the Germans.

PHILIP JACOB SPENER, the leader of the Pietists in Germany became pastor of the Lutheran Church of Frankford on the Main in the year 1666.

The dreadful effects of the Thirty Years' War, with following train of woes, was weighing heavily upon its the German church and the thoughts of the people were in a transition state, in which the warm life of practical religion was endeavoring to drive out and supersede the cold dead formalism of the preceding periods. Spener was a man splendidly endowed with intellectual, oratorical and spiritual faculties—just what was needed in this crisis of the history of the church—and in becoming the pastor of the church in Frankfort, he at once endeavored to carry out the lofty ideas of the purity and usefulness of the office he held, aiming at nothing less than a reproduction of the church as portrayed in the epistles of Paul. This would necessitate a reformation of church life throughout the entire country, as his course awakened the enmity and opposition of those who were satisfied with the prevailing tone of church life.

He also set up what were called "conventicles," or more properly, conferences of christians respecting matters of religion, in which they engaged in conversation on religious topics, instead of on other topics, and the nickname of Pietists was given these godly men, by those who derided them on account of their peculiar views. But this movement became a great power in awakening a spirit of evangelism throughout the country, and many noble men, preachers, professors and those in humble stations in life followed the guidance of this sincere exponent of divine truth. In the year 1677 William Penn, in company with George Fox, Robert Barclay, George Keith and others made an extensive proselyting tour through Germany, and met there Pietists, with whom they exchanged opinions on the work that was before them.

The followers of these Quakers were called "A new brood of fanatical spirits," but among the Mennonites of Germany they found kindred spirits, and in fact agreement in the salient points of Christian life and duty. "Both laid the greatest stress on inward piety, and a godly, humble life, considered all strife and warfare as unchristian, scrupulously abstained from making oath, declared against a paid ministry, exercised through their meetings a strict discipline over their members, favored silent prayer, were opposed to infant baptism, and looked upon the established churches as unhallowed vessels of the divine wrath."

It was to these people particularly that Penn and his companions directed their mission. They found severe laws against them on the statute book, and in many places they were persecuted by the people.

For a long time they had been looking toward America for a refuge from persecutions, and now Penn leads them more thoroughly to consider the propriety of crossing the sea and beginning life anew, in a land of religious freedom where there were no established churches and no foes to persecute. Penn at this time was thirty-three years of age, and captivating in his manner, and his heart was thoroughly aroused in behalf of those who for conscience sake endured persecution, so he comforted the brethren, told them of America, invited them to turn toward that land, and thus sent a thrill of hope throughout the homes and in the hearts of all the oppressed for religion's sake in the German fatherland.

Let us for a moment look at this remarkable man and thus we will the better understand his work.

William Penn was born in London, October 14, 1644. His father was a vice-admiral, a politician who with considerable skill preserved the favor of the ruling power. He was a man of great ambition and had marked out for his son a career of honor and usefulness to the state. Lady Penn, his wife, was as quiet and domestic as her husband was gay and worldly, and their son William inherited the religious traits of the mother's character, which grew with his growth and strengthened with his strength. As a consequence the boy early manifested the bent of his mind to the anger and consternation of the father, who turned him out of doors, punished him in various ways, surrounded him with contrary company, and did all he could to turn the boy into his own way of thinking, but it was useless, for his son was just as obstinate as himself. Penn happened to hear Thomas Loe, a Quaker preacher, speak on the words "There is a faith which overcometh the world, and there is a faith which is overcome by the world," and from this time he united himself heartily with this persecuted people.

William Penn was a man of rare power. He defied the authorities by his eloquent addresses, his fervid books, his court friendships and spotless character, and as a champion undertook the defence of his chosen associates. "He was an English gentleman, fond of dress, comfort, ease, and something like luxury, an accomplished courtier, a thorough business man, and one of the shrewdest students and judges of character." He was thoroughly acquainted with the ways and forms of royal courts, and could without the sacrifice of his principles make himself agreeable to those who held the sway in the land. Much more gifted in graces of intellect than his co-religionists he soon became the shaper of their ways, and thus led them out of many of their extravagances into a very staid and sober habit of life.

But the principles of the sect were very dear to him, and in seeking for kindred spirits he became acquainted with Spener and the Pietists of Germany, as also the Mennonites, German Quakers, Dunkards or German Baptists, and the hosts still within the Lutheran and Reformed Churches who prayed for the incoming of a better and truer religious life. It was a time of persecution, and the darkness was increasing, but God did not leave his people without a refuge. George Fox had visited America in 1671, but even in the New World the face of the people was sternly set against the Quakers. At length the opportunity opened to establish a refuge for the oppressed. In 1675 Edward Byllinge bought of Lord John Berkeley for £1000, one undivided half of New Jersey. Under this indirect purchase misunderstandings arose, but they were managed by the arbitration of William Penn, to whom, with two others, Byllinge assigned his property for the benefit of his creditors, on account of his failure. The nine-tenths of Byllinge's share, that is the one half of New Jersey, was offered for sale in decimal shares of tenths and hundredths; to carry out the purpose of an asylum for the persecuted, these shares were largely taken by Quakers. The part of the State thus allotted to the Quakers was West Jersey, the line of division running from Egg Harbor to a point on the Delaware River, under the forty-first degree of north latitude and near Burlington.

Now the Quakers had the opportunity for forming a government, and in 1677, the very year Penn was offering this asylum to the persecuted Germans, it was announced "We lay a foundation for after ages to understand their liberty as Christians and as men, that they might not be brought into bondage, but by their own consent, for we put *the power in the people.*"

"Freedom of conscience, the ballot box, equality before the law, the right of assembly, freedom of the press, popular sovereignty, trial by jury, open courts, free legislatures, this was the kind of a State in which refuge was offered the oppressed. Thus in New Jersey Penn's model of a state first found form."

Across the river was a large tract of land upon which several colonies of Swedes and Dutch had settled, the first colony arriving in 1638, the Swedes coming as permanent settlers, while the Dutch were adventurers, fond of trading and navigation, who came without their families to secure furs and pelts.

When Admiral Penn died, a part of the wealth he left his son was a claim against King Charles' Government for money lent, which with interest amounted to £15,000. But now the King had neither money nor credit, and this proved to be the opportunity of Penn to carry out his purpose of a state, an holy experiment, in which the question of religious freedom might be fully tested, so that he petitioned the King to grant him, in lieu of the £15,000, a tract of country in America, north of Maryland, with the Delaware on the east, its western limits the same as those of Maryland, and its northern as far as plantable country extended. This petition was received June 14, 1680. "It stated that the object of the petition was not only to provide a peaceful home for the persecuted members of the Society of Friends, but to afford an asylum for the good and oppressed of every nation on a basis of a practical application of the pure and peaceable principles of christianity."

As was to be expected this was strenuously opposed, and Penn's theories were by many held to be Utopian and dangerous alike to church and state, but Penn's friends prevailed, and on March 4, 1681, the King signed the desired grant, the King himself giving the territory the name Pennsylvania. At this time Penn was 37 years of age, and happy in having the greatest desires of his life thus far granted.

This and the following year were occupied with the most arduous labors. He at once sent out a deputy to act as his representative in Pennsylvania until his arrival, to get possession of the province as speedily as possible, to insure the allegiance of the the people, secure the revenue, and prepare the way for Penn.

Now Penn largely advertised his province, setting forth its attractive features, its opportunities to settlers, and its prospects for future growth. He also stated and had circulated ample information regarding the expense of emigration and settling, with instructions as to what people should take with them, in short, wise statesman that he was, he sought to turn the eyes of all Europe to his colony as the best and most desirable on the face of the earth. Thus he labored, securing emigrants, selling tracts of land, and preparing for his own departure.

On the 1st of September, 1682, in the ship "Welcome," three hundred tons, he embarked at Deal with a large company of Quakers, and arrived at New Castle on the Delaware, October 27, 1682.

Penn was at this time 38 years of age, still young, graceful, athletic, enthusiastic, still fond of boating and riding. Mr. J. F. Fisher thus describes him, " The true costume of the figure would have been that in vogue towards the end of the reign of Charles II This (as nearly as I can ascertain) was a collarless coat, perfectly straight in front, with many buttons, showing no waist, nor cut into skirts, having only a short buttoned slit behind, the sleeves hardly descending below the elbow, and having large cuffs, showing the full shirt sleeves. The vest was as long as the coat, and, except as to the sleeves, made apparently in the same way. The breeches were very full, open at the sides, and tied with strings." Penn was very particular as to his hat and wig, and wore a pair of leather stockings.

Penn's first experience in Pennsylvania is thus described, "It was the second week in November when the 'Welcome's' passengers landed, and the winds must have already been bleak and cutting, with now and then a film of ice or a flurry of snow, to prevent them from forgetting that winter was about to come. The first purchasers (and others who came over at this time) were nearly all Quakers, well to do people at home, who had sold their property in England and sought refuge in America to escape the prosecutions that had been visited upon them so often and so severely. They had servants, and were well supplied with clothing and provisions. Some of them were delicately nurtured women and children, unused to hardships of any kind. To such persons there would have been nothing romantic and nothing inviting in the prospect of a winter camp-meeting on the banks of the Delaware. The woods and swamps were so deep and thick between the two rivers that a span of hobbled horses lost there were not recovered for several months. There were no roads, scarcely paths, and the low houses of the Swedes and the lodges of the Indians were few and far apart. But the Quakers were a patient, long-suffering people, and the lofty woods of Coaquanock afforded at least a far better lodging place than the loathsome jails of England, in which many of them had languished. The air was pure, the water was clear and good, and the hearts of the adventurers beat high with hope. Their arms were strong, and they had good teachers in the Swedes, and the wood was plenty, both for fuel and other purposes, and every one had his axe and his spade."

"Some dug holes and caves in the dry banks of the two rivers, propped the superincumbent earth up with timbers, and, hanging their pots and kettles on improvised stakes and hooks at the entrances, speedily had warm and comparatively comfortable lodgings in the style of what hunters used to call 'half-faced camps.' Others rolled together forty or fifty logs, notched them at each end, and aided by their neighbors, could in a day or two, erect 'log cabins,' and these, roofed over with poles, upon which a thatch of bark from dead and fallen trees was laid, and the interstices between the logs 'chinked' with stones, mud, and clay, made residences which, in some sections of the country, are still thought to be good enough for any body. Others made more primitive huts still of stakes, bark, and brushwood, such as the savages sometimes toss together for their summer lodgings. The settlers had blankets and warm clothes in abundance, and we may suppose that the furs which the Indians brought in were in ready demand. With all these rude resources, we may safely believe that the early adventurers on the Delaware got through their first winter without much suffering or many deaths. There was no such distress as at Jamestown or at Plymouth. While their dwellings were not of the kind they had been accustomed to, it made but little difference to them because of the deep satisfaction with the religious liberty they enjoyed."

"Free from the presence and threats of their oppressors they could worship God as they chose, and in their worship found sufficient delights to take away the regrets for the lack of outward comforts. Hope spread her wings over them, and they joyfully looked for the coming of a brighter day when the birds would come back from the South, and the flowers peeping forth from their hiding places would greet the newly born verdure of meadows and trees."

Chapter III.

The Germans, and the Founding of Germantown.

IN the same year that Penn took possession of his Province, the work which he had done in his preaching tour through Germany, five years before, bore fruit. Eight German mystics or Mennonites, Penn's converts, formed a company which they called the Frankfort company, who purchased 25,000 acres of land in Pennsylvania, resolving to transport themselves and their families to that place. Their account of this purchase, and their enthusiasm awakened the enthusiasm of Francis Daniel Pastorius, a young man of thirty-one years of age, who determined that he would also go to the New World.

Pastorius was a man of good family of official standing; he was well acquainted with the classical languages, and with French, Dutch, English and Italian. He had been educated at the University of Strasburg, the High school of Basle, and the Law school of Jena. He began the practice of law in Frankfort, then traveled for two years in Holland, England, France, Switzerland and his own country. He was a prolific writer, a school teacher, a poet, historian, humorist, and was the possessor of fine administrative ability. He sailed from London for Philadelphia on June 10th, 1683. He became the founder of Germantown.

On June 11th, 1683, Penn sold 1000 acres of land each to Govert Remke, Lenart Arets, and Jacob Isaacs Von Bebber, a baker, all of Crefeld. It was from Crefeld that the first impulse to German emigration was given.

Crefeld was a town on the Rhine, close to the Netherland country. It was a population embracing many weavers and craftsmen, and among these many Quakers and Mennonites who had been the victims of persecution.

In his visit of 1677 Penn preached to them and aroused their hope for a land of liberty, and now that he had purchased the Province, he sells the land to them that they desired. He sold to Jacob Telner, Jans Strypers, and Dirch Sipman, of Crefeld, each 5000 acres in the Province. The most of the colony that came from Crefeld were weavers, and sending Pastorius to select their lands for them, he came, obtained the tract, named it Germanopolis, and then it was called Germantown and is so called to-day. "From that time many came to the land of freedom, and Germantown grew, sent out offshoots, had its representatives in the Assembly—Pastorius and Abraham Opden Graeff—was incorporated as a borough in 1681, with Pastorius for bailiff, Telner and others, burgesses, etc., and had power to hold a court and market, lay fines, and enact ordinances. The people were called together once a year and had the laws read to them."

Loher says of the people, "They would do nothing but work and pray, and their mild conscience made them opposed to the swearing of oaths and courts, and would not suffer them to use harsh weapons against thieves and trespassers."

But they were diligent workers, and their fine linen was highly valued. So many of them were spinners that Pastorius in devising a town seal, selected a trefoil of clover, one leaf bearing a vine, one a stalk of flax, the third a weaver's spool, with the motto, *Vinum, Linum, et Textrinum*.

When William Penn arrived in 1682 not more than a few wigwams, and not over twenty houses, were on the present site of the city of Philadelphia, while on the eastern side of the Delaware, from Salem to Trenton there were not more than 3,500 white inhabitants. In two years the population of Philadelphia had increased to 2,500, and trade had been established with England, the West Indies, South America, and the Mediterranean.

In the year 1699 Philadelphia had a population of 5000, and the Province more than 20,000, the most of whom were the victims of persecution in England, Wales, France, Germany and other countries of Europe.

Laurens Hendricks, one of the Germans, says of his people, "They were naturally very rugged people, who could endure much hardships; they wore long unshaven beards, disordered clothing, great shoes, which were heavily hammered with iron and large nails; they lived in the mountains of Switzerland, far from cities and towns, with little intercourse with other men; their speech is rude and uncouth, and they have difficulty in understanding any one who does not speak just their way; they are very zealous to serve God with prayer and reading and in other ways, and very innocent in all their doings as lambs and doves."

While this might describe some, it would not describe all who were Germans in the settlements.

The Germans started from Germantown as their headquarters, and went north into the interior; the Welsh south of the Schuylkill, while the Quakers still south of them, also between the German settlements on the north and the Delaware, as also forming the greater number of the inhabitants in the city of Philadelphia. "Of these Swiss emigrants just described, it is recorded in their records, how, after they had decided to emigrate, they returned to the Palatinate to seek their wives and children, who are scattered everywhere in Switzerland, in Alsace and in the Palatinate, and *they know not where they are to be found.*"

Pastorius used a cave as his first habitation, and it was in this cave in 1683 that the apportionment of lots in Germantown was made. Pastorius then built himself a small cabin thirty feet long, eighteen feet broad with a partition near the middle. This house was furnished with windows of oiled paper.

In 1685 the town was laid out, and running through it was a street sixty feet wide. This street followed an Indian trail, and on each side were very thick woods inhabited by bears and other wild animals.

In 1700 this street for the distance of a mile was lined on each side with peach trees in full bearing. The houses of the settlers were, each one, surrounded with a garden, while such enterprising men as Rittenhouse, Robeson, Dewees, etc., established mills along the wild and romantic Wissahickon.

In building their houses the Germans built with one chimney in the center of the building, which was different from that of all other settlers. They used great porcelain stoves, such as they had used in their former homes, until Christopher Saur, the Germantown printer, invented the ten-plate stove. There were no carpets of any kind, but in the plainest way they lived, priding themselves on the abundance of clothing they owned, and on the heartiness with which they ate their food.

William Penn established annual fairs to encourage the people in the quality of their productions, and in 1686 it is recorded that Abraham Opden Graeff, of Germantown, petitioned Council to grant him the Governor's premium for the first and finest piece of linen cloth.

One item of history should be recorded as one of many evidences of the clear ideas of right and wrong held by these Germantown settlers. "In 1688 Pastorious, Opden Graeff, and Gerhardt Hendricks sent to the Friend's Meeting House the first public protest ever made on this continent against the holding of slaves, or, as they uncompromisingly styled it, 'the traffic of men's body.' They compare negro slavery to slavery under Turkish pirates, and cannot see that one is better than the other. 'There is a saying that we shall doe to all men licke as we will be done ourselves; making no difference of what generation, descent, or colour they are, and those who steal or robb men, and those who buy or purchase them, are they not all alicke? Here is liberty of conscience wch is right and reasonable; here ought to be lickewise liberty of ye body, except of evil doers, wch is another case. In Europe there are many oppressed for conscience sake; and here are those oppressed wch die of a black colour.'"

"The Germans asked, 'Have these negroes not as much right to fight for their freedom as you have to keep them slaves?' and asked further to be informed what right Christians have to maintain slavery, 'to the end we shall be satisfied in this point and satisfie likewise our good friends and acquaintances in our natif country, to whom it is a terrour or fairfull thing that men should be handled so in Pennsylvania.' The Quakers were embarrassed by the memorial, and its blunt style of interrogatory. It was submitted to the Monthly Meeting, inspected and found weighty, passed to the Quarterly Meeting, then recommended to the Yearly Meeting, which, meeting at Burlington, backed down from a clear decision by reporting it 'not to be so proper for this meeting to give a positive judgment in the case. It having so general a relation to many other parts, and therefore, at present, they forebore it.' So the matter slept."

In Germantown, the law courts descended to some very minute matters in order to preserve the moral tone of the community. As an example, "Peter Keurlis, charged with not coming when the justices sent for him, with refusing to lodge travelers, with selling barley-malt at four pence per quart, and of violating Germantown law by selling more than a gill of rum and a quart of beer every half-day to each individual.' Peter's answer was, 'He did not come because he had much work to do; he did not entertain travelers because he only sold drink and did not keep an ordinary. He knew nothing about the four pence a quart law of the Province, and as for the Germantown statute, the people he sold to being able to bear more, he could not or would not obey the law.' He lost his license. For calling hard names, calling a witch, cheating, swearing, dancing after ten o'clock at night, women dressing in men's apparel, and such like offenders, were sent to the house of correction or the ducking stool.

In 1704 William Dewees was Constable in Germantown, and it was his duty to be very careful in guarding against the breaking of the law. In 1706 he was the Sheriff of the town.

William Penn's invitation to the Germans to settle in his province was so gladly received by them, that every year large shiploads came, and the people dispersed themselves throughout the back country, until the English people became alarmed. They were afraid of being out-voted in the control of the Province. They were afraid that the whole tone of the Province would be changed from what it had originally been intended. Hence the effort was made to restrict emigration, and all after September, 1727, were marched in line to the court house where they laid down their guns, met the Governor, subscribed the oaths, saluted the Governor with three volleys, the same to the Mayor and Sheriff, and so back to the ship.

Douglas, the historian, in 1755, says, "This colony, by importation of foreigners and other strangers in very great numbers, grows prodigiously; by their laborious and penurious manner of living, they grow rich where others starve and by their superior industry and frugality may in time drive out the British people from the colony."

The extent of the German immigration was indeed surprising, for several years it averaged 2000 a year, and they came not as paupers, but with money to purchase lands and with strong frame and hopeful hearts to build their homes. The persecution they had endured in Germany no doubt made them wary, and the strangeness of their language made them clannish, so that a false impression was created in regard to them in the minds of the English, and that impression remains even to this present day. History written by the English has misrepresented them persistently, and only now when the records are searched can we see the real power and virtue of these noble Germans, who for conscience sake left their homes and builded anew in the American forests.

It is difficult at this day to determine what was the main reason prompting the impolitic and strange conduct of the assembly of the Province toward the immigrants from the Palatinate. In one year from December 1728 to December 1729 over 6000 emigrants came, but the greater number of these were from Ireland, but the report was that a great number would come from the Palatinate the following year. Hence the assembly made haste to enact the law laying a duty of forty shillings per head on all aliens imported. Gordon suggests that the reason of this law may have been to increase the revenue of the Province.

He says, "In justice to the Germans, it should be told that this law was enacted in the face of a report of a committee of the house, containing satisfactory evidence of their good conduct. 'The Palatines who had been imported directly into the Province, had purchased and honestly paid for their lands, had conducted thamselves respectably towards the government, paid their taxes readily, and were a sober and honest people in their religious and civil duties. Yet some who had come by the way of New York, and elsewhere, had seated themselves on lands of the proprietaries and others, and refused to yield obedience to the government.' "

The early settlers of Germantown were not only distinguished for their excellent weaving, but also for their love of learning. We have seen that Pastorious was a fine scholar, and we will see that in this he was not an exception, nor was he without congenial associates in this settlement.

The Germans soon laid hold of the printing press, and with characteristic religious zeal made a specialty of printing the Word of God. They felt that their freedom depended upon a general adherence to that Word. They loved it, believed it, rejoiced in it, and no household could be counted as complete without a copy of that Word. Hence one of the earliest triumphs in art by the Germans of Germantown was the printing of the Bible, in which all the mechanical work was done by themselves, and that specimen of their skill to-day is an honor to their zeal and thorough workmanship.

A DELAWARE INDIAN.

Chapter IV.

The Indians.

THE vastness of the forests impressed the colonists with a dread of the peculiar and mysterious people who dwelt in them, and immigration aided largely in forming a judgment of these future neighbors. Their manners were so different that it was almost impossible to do them justice, for the only standard by which they could be tried was the European. There was a great misconception as to their numbers. They did not dwell in great swarms, nor rove in large armies, nor dwell in large cities. The Indians were really few in number. "In 1665 there were only 11,750, all told, of Iroquois, 2,350 of them being warriors, and these required 60,000 square miles for their hunting grounds. The Susquehannas never had more than 8,000 souls. The Canada Hurons never exceeded 20,000 in all. The most populous branch of the Algonquins, the Mohegans of New York and New England, Parkman commutes could not have had more than 8000 fighting men, or 40,000 in all. The Lenapes of Pennsylvania and New Jersey could scarcely have reached half so many. Gordon thinks that at the most populous period there must have been less than 47,000 Indians within the limits of Pennsylvania."

It is interesting to read Penn's description of them, "They are generally tall, straight in their persons, well built, and of singular proportion; they tread strong and clever, and mostly walk with a lofty chin. Of complexion black, but by design as the gypsies in England. They grease themselves with bear's fat clarified, and using no defence against sun and weather, their skins must needs be swarthy. Their eye is livid and black, not unlike a straight looked Jew. The thick lips and flat nose, so frequent with the East Indians and blacks, are not common to them, for I have seen as comely European-like faces among them, of both sexes, as on your side the sea; and truly an Italian complexion hath not more of the white; and the noses of several of them have as much of the Roman. Their language is lofty yet narrow; but, like the Hebrew, in signification, full. Like shorthand in writing, one word serveth in the place of three, and the rest are supplied by the understanding of the hearer; imperfect in their tenses, wanting in their moods, participles, adverbs, conjunctions, and interjections. I have made it my business to understand it, that I might not want an interpreter on any occasion; and I must say that I know not a language spoken in Europe that hath words of more sweetness or greatness, in accent and emphasis, than theirs. For instance, Octokekon, Rançocas, Oricton, Shak, Marian, Poquesian, all of which are names of places, and have grandeur in them. Of words of sweetness, *anna* is mother; *issimus*, a brother; *netcap*, friend; *usqueoret*, very good; *pave*, bread; *metsa*, eat; *mattu*, no; *hatta*, to have; *payo*, to come; Sepassen, Passijon, the names of places; Tamane, Secane, Menanse, Secataseus, are the names of persons. If we ask them for anything they have not, they will answer, *mattu ne hatta*, which, to translate, is 'not I have,' instead of 'I have not.'

"Of their customs and manners there is much to be said. I will begin with children. So soon as they are born they are washed in water, and while very young and in cold weather to choose, they plunge them in the river to harden and embolden them. Having wrapped them in a clout they lay them on a straight thin board a little more than the length and breadth of the child, and swaddle it fast upon the board to make it straight; wherefore all Indians have flat heads; and thus they carry them at their backs. The children will go (walk) very young, at nine months commonly. They wear only a small clout around their waist till they are big. If boys, they go a fishing till ripe for the woods, which is about fifteen. There they hunt, and having given some proofs of their manhood by a good return of skins, they marry; else it is shame to think of a wife. The girls stay with their mothers, and help to hoe the ground, plant corn, and carry burdens; and they do well to use them to that, while young, which they must do when they are old; for the wives are the true servants of the husbands; otherwise the men are very affectionate to them. When the young women are fit for marriage they wear something upon their heads for an advertisement, but so as their faces are hardly to be seen but when they please. The age they marry at, if women, is about thirteen or fourteen, if men seventeen or eighteen. They are rarely older. Their houses are mats or barks of trees, set on poles in the fashion of an English barn, but out of the power of the winds, for they are hardly higher than a man. They lie on reeds or grass. In travel they lodge in the woods about a great fire, with the mantle of duffils they wear by day wrapt about them and a few boughs stuck round them. Their diet is maize, or Indian corn, divers ways prepared, sometimes roasted in the ashes, sometimes beaten and boiled with water, which they call *homine*. They also make cakes not unpleasant to eat. They have likewise several sorts of beans and peas that are good nourishment, and the woods and rivers owe their larder. If an European comes to see them or calls for lodging at their house or wigwam, they give him the best place and first cut. If they come to visit us they salute us with an Itah! which is as much as to say, 'Good be to you!' and set them down, which is mostly on the ground, close to their heels, their legs upright; it may be they speak not a word, but observe all that passes. If you give them anything to eat or drink, well, for they will not ask; and, be it little or much, if it be with kindness, they are well pleased; else they go away sullen, but say nothing. They are great concealers of their own resentments, brought to it, I believe, by the revenge that hath been practiced among them. In either of these they are not exceeded by the Italians.

"In liberality they excel; nothing is too good for their friend; give them a fine gun, coat, or other thing, it may pass through twenty hands before it sticks; light of heart, strong affections, but soon spent. The most merry creatures that live, feast and dance perpetually; they never have much, nor never want much; wealth circulateth like the blood; all parts partake, and though none shall want what another hath, yet exact observers of property. Some Kings have sold, others presented me with several parcels of land; the pay or presents I made them were not hoarded by the particular owners: but the neighboring Kings and their clans being present when the goods were brought out, the parties chiefly concerned consulted what and to whom they should give them. To every King then, by the hands of a person for that work appointed, is a proportion sent, so sorted and folded, and with that gravity that is admirable. Then that King subdivideth it in like manner among his dependents, they hardly leaving themselves an equal share with one of their subjects ; and be it on such occasions or festivals, or at their common meals, the Kings distribute, and to themselves last.

"They care for little, because they want but little ; and the reason is, a little contents them. In this they are sufficiently revenged on us ; if they are ignorant of our pleasures, they are also free from our pains. Since the Europeans came into these parts they are grown great lovers of strong liquors, rum especially, and for it they exchange the richest of their skins and furs. If they are heated with liquors they are restless till they have enough to sleep, that is their cry, *some more and I will go to sleep;* but when drunk one of the most wretched spectacles in the world. In sickness, impatient to be cured ; and for it give anything, especially for their children, to whom they are extremely natural. They drink at these a *tisan*, or decoction of some roots in spring water ; and if they eat any flesh it must be of the female of any creature. If they die they bury them with their apparel, be they man or woman, and the nearest of kin fling in something precious with them as a token of their love. Their mourning is blacking of their faces, which they continue for a year. They are choice of the graves of their dead, for, lest they should be lost by time and fall to common use, they pick off the grass that grows upon them, and heap up the fallen earth with great care and exactness. These poor people are under a dark night in things relating to religion; to be sure the tradition of it; yet they believe a God and immortality without the help of metaphysics, for they say, 'There is a Great King that made them, who dwells in a glorious country to the southward of them, and that the souls of the good shall go thither where they shall live again.' Their worship consists of two parts, sacrifice and cantico. Their sacrifice is their first fruits; the first and fattest buck they kill goeth to the fire, where he is all burnt, with a mournful ditty of him that performeth the ceremony, but with such marvellous fervency and labor of body that he will even sweat to a foam. The other part is their cantico, performed by round dances, sometimes words, sometimes songs, then shouts, two being in the middle that begin, and by singing and dancing on a board direct the chorus. Their postures in the dance are very antick and different, but all keep measure. This is done with equal earnestness and labor, but great appearance of joy.

"In the Fall when the corn cometh in, they begin to feast one another. There have been two great feasts already, to which all come that will. I was at one myself; their entertainment was a great seat by a spring under some shady trees, and twenty bucks with hot cakes of new corn, both wheat and beans, which they made up in a square form in the leaves of the stem and bake them in the ashes, and after that they fall to dance. But they that go must carry a small present in their money; it may be sixpence, which is made of the bone of a fish; the black is with them as gold, the white silver; they call it wampum. Their government is by kings, which they call Sachama, and these by succession, but always on the mother's side. The reason they render for this way of descent is, that their issue may not be spurious. Every king hath his council, and that consists of all the old and wise men of the nation, which perhaps is 200 people. Nothing of moment is undertaken, be it war, peace, selling of land, or traffic, without advising with them, and, which is more with the young men too. It is admirable to consider how powerful the kings are, and yet how they move by the breath of their people. I have had occasion to be in council with them upon treaties of land, and to adjust the terms of trade. Their order is thus: The king sits in the middle of an half moon, and hath his council, the old and wise on each hand; behind them, or at a little distance, sit the younger fry in the same figure. Having consulted and resolved their business, the king ordered one of them to speak to me; he stood up, came to me, and, in the name of his king, saluted me; then took me by the hand and told me,

He was ordered by his king to speak to me, and that now it was not he, but the king that spoke; because what he should say was the king's mind.' He first prayed me 'to excuse them, that they had not complied with me last time, he feared there might be some fault in the interpreter, being neither Indian nor English; besides, it was the Indian custom to deliberate and take up much time in council before they resolve, and that if the young people and owners of the land had been as ready as he, I had not met with so much delay.' Having thus introduced his matter, he fell to the bounds of the land they had agreed to dispose of and the price, which now is little and dear, that which would have bought twenty miles not buying now two. During the time that this man spoke not a man of them was seen to whisper or smile, the old grave, the young reverent in their deportment. They speak little, but fervently and with elegance. I have never seen more natural sagacity, considering them without the help of tradition, and he will deserve the name of wise that outwits them in any treaty about a thing they understand."

Penn thus presents the most favorable phase of their character. He always found them to be honorable and trusty, and they deeply reverenced him. He never saw the bursting forth of the darker side of their nature, so familiar a little more than half a century afterward.

Charles Thomas, who had the best of opportunities for observing them, says "They were perfect strangers to the use of iron. The instruments with which they dug up the ground were of wood, or a stone fastened to a handle of wood. Their hatchets for cutting were of stone, sharpened to an edge by rubbing, and fastened to a wooden handle. Their arrows were pointed with flint or bone. What clothing they wore was of the skins of animals taken in hunting, and their ornaments were principally of feathers. They all painted or daubed their faces with red. . The men suffered only a tuft of hair to grow on the crown of their head; the rest, whether on their head or faces, they prevented from growing by constantly plucking it out by the roots, so they always appeared as if they were bald and beardless. Many were in the habit of marking their faces, arms, and breast by picking the skin with thorns and rubbing the parts with a fine powder made of charcoal, which, penetrating the punctures left an indelible stain or mark, which remained as long as they lived. The punctures were made in figures according to their several fancies. The only part of the body which they covered was from the waist half way down to the thighs, and their feet they guarded with a kind of shoe made of hides of buffaloes or deerskin, laced tight over the instep and up to the ankles with thongs. It was and still continues to be a common practice among the men to slit their ears, putting something into the hole to prevent its closing, and then by hanging weights to the lower part to stretch it out, so that it hangs down the cheek like a large ring. They had no knowledge of the use of silver and gold. Instead of money they used a kind of beads made of conch shells manufactured in a curious manner. These beads were made, some of the white, some of the black or colored parts of the shell. They were formed into cylinders about one quarter of an inch long and were a quarter of an inch in diameter. They were round and highly polished and perforated lengthwise with a small hole, by which they strung them together and wove them into belts, some of which, by a proper arrangement of the beads of different colors, were figured like carpetting with different figures according to the various uses for which they were designed. These were made use of in their treaties and intercourse with each other, and served to assist their memory and preserve the remembrance of transactions. When different tribes or nations made peace or alience with each other they exchanged belts of one sort. Hence they were distinguished by the name of peace or war belts. Every messenger sent from one tribe to another was accompanied with a string of these beads or a belt, and the string or belt was smaller or greater according to the weight and importance of the subject. These beads were their riches. They were worn as bracelets and like chains round the neck by way of ornament."

It is interesting to know how, when the medium of exchange among them was so different from that of the settlers, they bargained.

"In 1677 a tract of land twenty miles square on the Delaware between Timber and Oldman's creek was purchased for the following: thirty match coats (made of hairy wool with the rough side out) twenty guns, thirty kettles, one great kettle, thirty pair of hose, twenty fathoms of duffels (Duffield blanket cloth of which match coats were made), thirty petticoats, thirty narrow hose, thirty bars of lead, fifteen small barrels of powder, seventy knives, thirty Ingian axes, seventy combs, sixty pairs of tobacco tongs, sixty pair of scissors, sixty tinshaw looking glasses, one hundred and twenty awl blades, one hundred and twenty fish hooks, two grasps of red paint, one hundred and twenty needles, sixty tobacco boxes, one hundred and twenty pipes, two hundred bells, one hundred jews harps, and anchors of rum."

Indian villages were few, far between, and small, but the forests were traversed on regularly established and well-known paths called trails. The footprint of an Indian could be at once recognized, for he always stepped with a perfectly straight foot, and without turning his toes out, so that if the sun was upon his back, the shadow of his shanks would entirely cover his feet. To the Indian the advantage of this was, he was able to walk more safely the narrow forest path, and to step also with greater stealth and softness in pursuit of his enemy and his game where leaves to rustle and twigs to break are numerous, and also to carry himself singularly straight, his shoulders never diverging from a perpendicular."

The huts of the Indians were so constructed that the smoke from the fire in the center of the hut went out of the top. In winter the atmosphere of these huts was of the most objectionable character to those not accustomed to it.

"The interior of the cabin was stained and dingy with smoke that could find no regular outlet, and it was so pungent and acrid as to cause much inflamation of the eyes, and blindness in old age. The fleas and other vermin were bad and the children were noisy and unruly beyond parallel, raising a pandemonium in each lodge, which the shrill shrieking of the Hecate like squaws added to without controlling it. Parkman draws a vivid picture of a lodge on a Winter night, lighted up by the uncertain flickers of resinous flames that sent fitful flashes through the dingy canopy of smoke, a bronzed group encircling the fire, cooking, eating, gambling, or amusing themselves with idle chaff; grizzly old warriors, scarred with the marks of repeated battles; shriveled squaws, hideous with toil and hardships endured for half a century; young warriors with a record to make, vain, boastful, obstreperous; giddy girls, gay with paint, ochre, wampum and braid; restless children, pell-mell with restless dogs."

Such were the strange people who hovered around the frontier settlements, gradually receding as the settlers advanced, but for the first century of the history of the Province the neighbors of the Europeans who in their wilderness, by the sacrifice of all the comforts of cultured society and European conveniences sought to established christian homes.

Chapter V.

Immigration and Settlement in the Wilderness.

> "Oh, say, why seek ye other lands?
> The Neckar's vale hath wine and corn;
> Full of dark firs the Schwarzwald stands;
> In Spessart-rings the Alp-herd's horn.
>
> Ah! in strange forests how ye'll yearn
> For the green mountains of your home,
> To Deutschland's yellow wheat-fields turn
> In spirit o'er the vine hills roam."
>
> FREILIGRATH.

IN the year 1701 William Penn issued Letter Patents granting to the Frankfort Company, composed of inhabitants of Frankfort on the Main, in Germany, and represented by their attorneys, Daniel Falkner and Johannes Jawert, a tract of land containing 22,377 acres and situated where the borough of Pottstown now stands and extending back into the country about twelve miles.

In 1708, Falkner, who resided in Germantown, granted this tract to John Henry Sprogell in consideration of the sum of £500, in the current money of Pennsylvania, which was paid in "silver coyne."

Sprogell cut up this vast domain into lots to suit purchasers, who were mostly merchants of Philadelphia, who purchased for speculation.

In the same manner the heirs of William Penn sold tracts lying east of the great tract. We cannot tell the dates in which the various leading men came to the American refuge. We do not know when William Dewees came, or whether his coming influenced Frederick Antes to come. Nor do we know just what year Frederick Antes came. We do know, however, that he came when his son Henry was closely approaching manhood, for he had been carefully instructed in the articles of the Reformed faith, by a competent master in the Fatherland. No longer a child, but able to weigh such matters seriously, he was undoubtedly filled with a spirit of enthusiasm such as has ever marked the German character when the deepest chords of their souls were touched.

All Germany was aroused by the reports of the agents of William Penn. Perhaps every ship that came had on board some one who would become important in the growth of the colony. It was now an unrecorded rush of emigrants, who came to make the most of the opportunities as they should open before them. And to-day their descendents are the bone and sinew of the State.

How beautiful was the Rhineland to these people as for the last time they gazed upon it, with its splendidly rolling hills, its steep bluffs, its majestic rivers, its hills crowned with ancient castles, large baronial halls and frowning fortresses; its green fields, extensive vineyards, and its noble forests; its cities with halls of learning, large and ornate cathedrals, palaces, and thousands of dwellings. All these were evidences of the growth of the civilization of the past, and now the demon of persecution had swooped down upon the land, and those who loved it the most, who hoped for its purest redemption, would only be permitted to remain there by bowing the neck to the conqueror, and robbing themselves of conscience. This they could not do. They had true hearts, and were fearless before the foe; sturdy and brave, they said " we will make a home in the distant wilderness, where we shall be free. God will be with us there, and we shall make that land as our own." Then came the march to the seaport, and the venturesome embarkation.

The young man Henry Antes was not only bold in heart, but intelligent also. He was well instructed in the faith, and could speak words of comfort and minister to the anxious ones in their sadness at the parting from home. They had no minister with them. It was a flock without a shepherd, but what mattered the forms and authority of ordination now, it was the spirit that made alive, and did it not dwell in the noble Henry, the sweet singer of Freinsheims.

The voyage in those days was long. Half a year often rolled away while the ship was breasting the billows. They were indeed at the mercy of the wind and the waves. Storms arose and beat upon them, the water and sky meeting all about them at times seemed to be in a conspiracy for their destruction. Sickness, too, entered their berths, even the dreadful small-pox scourge beset them. Many of their loved ones were cast overboard into the watery grave, which by its ceaseless motion sung the refrain, "No rest, no rest," while the sharks, with cruel, rapacious eyes, followed the vessel to rob the ocean of its prey.

We can imagine Henry Antes with the fervor of youth, and the zeal of the martyr, standing before them and comforting them Only a full heart could give comfort at such a time, and his heart was full.

He was strong in body, large in size, brave in manner, inspiring in presence, and quick to perceive the needs of the hour. And when he led the evening song, as the sun went down out of the sky into the sea before them, his fervent faith led them all to hope on, and pray on until the sun would no longer go down into the sea, but into the bosom of their own adopted homes.

At last land was reached, and the broad river entered, and on either shore they beheld the woods stretching far away in the distance from the waters edge. But it was not like their own Rhineland, here it was level, or but slightly elevated.

And as they watched these wild forest-crowned shores, the city of Penn, the end of their sea journey, appeared before them. But how strangely different from the cities they had left.

No cathedrals, no palaces, no great castles, no stone structures telling of the wars of man for full five hundred years, no great crowds of moving throngs, no soldiers in glittering array, no shout of thousands, no rushing to and fro, only a few hundred small houses scattered upon the hill by the bank of the river, and a number of quiet looking people who in a strange plain dress came down to the water's edge to see them, greet them, and bid them welcome to their city. These were the Quakers, the followers of William Penn into the wilderness home, and the people whose honesty and peaceful conduct won the confidence and the respect of all the Indians of the forest. Their language was strange to the coming immigrants, but their manners plainly conveyed their meaning.

Back of the city in every direction the low hills were covered with forests. These forests stretched over the great continent. Within them roamed numerous tribes of savage Indians, within them also lurked the bear, the panther, the wildcat, the stag, the wolf, and many smaller and less dangerous animals. The forests were well stocked with game, the streams with fish, the undergrowth with birds.

Here indeed was the opportunity for the father to provide for his little ones, and they rejoiced at the thought that they could make these forests primeval ring with the melody of their sacred songs as they rejoiced in their religious freedom, and not fear the approach of a foe.

In Mahanitania was an immense tract of land embracing more than 22,000 acres. In this tract the ax of the settler had not yet been heard. It was a large hollow basin and afterwards was known as the Schwam (meadows). In this tract many of these persons were to find their way, but now they went only to the high hills back of the Quaker City, on the level lands above the Wissahickon, and there on the ascending ranges, swung their axes and built their cabins, within easy reach of the settlement at Germantown.

One of those that had come over with the earlier refugees from the Palatinate was William Dewees of the manufacturing town of Crefeld, on the Rhine.

In the church Frederick Antes, the father of Henry Antes, and William Dewees were elders, to whom the body looked for guidance and counsel. But early in their acquaintance Henry Antes found a greater attraction in Christina, the daughter of William Dewees, who was not at all averse to the attentions he bestowed upon her.

In the arrangements of the colony, William Dewees and his family remained in Germantown, and by the banks of the Wissahickon built a paper mill, and gathered his workmen around and called his new home after his old home, by the familiar title Crefeld. But Frederick Antes with his household went farther into the forests and in Falkner swamp, a part of the Mahanatania tract of 25,000 acres, chose his home, and gathered about him the bolder ones who were not afraid of the wilderness.

In this the real spirit of the ardent young Henry Antes found full play, and he delighted in the opportunities it gave him to lay a foundation for his own future home.

Though in appearance he was a big burly German farmer, in reality he was a man of faculties far above his surroundings.

As a mechanic, with a quick eye and a ready hand, he could do his work in a manner that found no superior. As a scholar he became the writer of the legal documents of all his countrymen in that section. As a hunter, he studied the haunts and habits of all the creatures he beheld in the woods. As a farmer he noted the qualities of the soil, and was able to point to the spot where in the future the best crops could be gathered. As a guide he learned every path of the forest and could follow a trail as surely as the Indians that dwelt near them, as a friend his counsel was wise and judicious, for he always sought for the guidance the eternal principles of truth and righteousness, and as the years passed on, he became the principal man of the community, and with the esteem and affection of the people gathered about him wealth and honor.

There was nothing elaborate in the dwellings of these settlers. All luxury in dwelling, furniture, clothing, and such like had been left on the other side of the sea. Hence their principal possession at the first was the ax to cut down the trees, build the log house, split the logs and hew them and make the furniture. It was the ring of the ax that made the music on every side. It was the ax that first was crowned conqueror and king.

What skill was here displayed! how varied the stroke as to the purpose in view! how the tight fitting logs proclaimed the skill of the builder! how the tables, the chairs, the bedsteads all revealed the accuracy of the stroke and marked the cabinet maker! Every house had a great wide door-way, through which a horse could be driven, dragging into the cabin the huge back-log for the fire-place; and the broad windows in which was placed oiled paper instead of glass. These people were hardy and lived mostly out of doors. They were not afraid of the sunshine or the winds, but inured to hardships delighted in their power to overcome the threatenings of the storms.

The first consideration was a good strong house,

with its fire-place covering an entire side of a room, a good spring of water near by, a running stream not far away, and a right to the acres of woodland about them, to clear for the coming crops. The fishing tackle they must all know how to use. The gun too must be familiar to man and woman. The men made their shoes, the women their clothes. The spinning-wheel stood beside every fire-place, and in the evenings its busy hum proclaimed the industry of the females.

They needed neither clock nor watch, for by the sun they told the time of day. They needed but few of the implements of civilization, for they cultivated their inventive faculties, and he who had the most talent was sure to reveal it in his dwelling. The family Bible and the hymn-book were sacred, and the life of the father was the guide for the son. In was in such a house and with such surroundings that Henry Antes began life in the land of the free and the home of the brave.

Those were the days of stalwart manhood, when a man was master of his surroundings. He was conqueror, and in every act and every step of his life showed his superiority over the forces of nature and the demands of society. The scream of the panther at night gave them no fear, for well they knew that before the unerring aim of their rifles it would be sure to fall. Nor did they fear the face of the Indian as he peered into their dwellings, for they trusted in their righteous dealings, giving a full equivalent for all they secured.

And then when the Sabbath came, from all the country round about they gathered together, and Henry Antes, the most scholarly among them, read to them the Word of God. Stalwart men knelt down on the grass by the creeks, or on the leaves of the grove, and in loud voices poured forth their prayers to God, while with one accord they all sung the songs of Zion, until the woods were made melodious with the sound. They sung the songs of the Fatherland, and then sent messages back over the sea to their kindred and friends telling them of the heart joys in the free, wild, pure life in the Western Wilderness.

Chapter VI.

Marriage of Henry Antes, and the Settlers of the New Country. Boehm's Administrations.

THE stroke of Henry Antes was the sturdier as the fair face of Christina Dewees flashed before him, and he searched over hill and dale for a place to build for her the cottage which should be of the best. In his rambles he came to the forks of the Perkeawming, and there saw the spot which was to be their home; to win it was the problem his earnest labor was to solve.

It was between thirty and forty miles from his father's house to Germantown, where Christina lived, but what was this distance when it was his love that called him? And we can readily imagine what his feelings must have been as he frequently traversed this distance.

The path lay along the top of the ridge, on the one side of which was the broken hill country, and on the other side flowed the Schuylkill. On his right he could see the broad valley with its many smaller streams emptying into the river, and on the left a wide rolling country, with here and there broad valleys and the Blue mountains in the distance enclosing them. Along this ridge he would come until he would strike the Wissahickon and between its battlements of hills he would pass until he would come to the ravine which led up to the house of his beloved.

In the gorge of the Wissahickon he met with some of the most interesting characters, who dwelt in these deep ravines, in intimate communion with their Lord, such men were John Seelig and Conrad Matthias. These men were led by John Kelpius, who died a few years before this time, but these two were his most faithful followers. John Kelpius, a man of remarkable brilliancy, was a noble of an eminent family in Siebenbergen. He was learned in Hebrew, Greek, Latin, German and English, and reasoned acutely and soberly. He died in the year 1708. Then Seelig took his place, and to specially distinguish himself wore, as his teacher had done, a very coarse garment. But his kindly offices were to all the people round-about, and many of the oldest deeds of conveyance of that neighborhood are in his hand-writing. When he died Matthias took his place as the teacher, and with him was associated Doctor Christopher Witt, and these, with their companions (there were forty-two at first), were called "The Society of the Woman of the Wilderness," spoken of in Revelation, and they as the beloved of the "Woman of the Wilderness" had become hermits, had laid aside all other engagements, and by adorning themselves with holiness were preparing for her reception, for which they looked daily.

"They called themselves 'The Society of the Woman in the Wilderness,' and they believed in the near approach of the millenium. They believed that the 'Woman in the Wilderness' mentioned in Revelation was prefigurative of the great deliverence of the church of Christ, then about to be displayed; that, as she was 'to come up from the Wilderness, leaning on her beloved,' so the beloved, becoming hermits, and laying aside all other engagements, should prepare for her reception, by adorning themselves with holiness; and should observe the signs of the times, if, peradventure, the 'Harbinger' might appear. They taught that there was a threefold wilderness state of progression in spiritual holiness; the barren, the fruitful, and the wilderness state of the elect of God; the last of which, the highest degree of holiness, was to be obtained by dwelling in solitude, in the wilderness. Thus Moses acquired his holiness by a preparation of forty years in the desert; and then St. John was qualified, and Christ himself was prepared by his forty days temptation in the wilderness; whence it was inferred, that holy men might be qualified to come forth again, to convert 'whole cities,' and to work signs and wonders. With more good sense than usually accompanied such vagaries, these holy men waited for some satisfactory evidence of their apostolic qualifications, which not receiving, they were content to instruct such only as sought their haunts."

Antes would certainly enjoy meeting these men, for they were greatly respected by the people of Germantown, and the memory of their learned leader was still cherished by the people who had been the recipients of his kindness, for, although they dwelt in the forests as hermits, they went about doing good, and seeking to manifest the spirit of Christ. They particularly sought out the sick, and helped them with the herbs they so well knew the virtue of, and the afflicted they comforted with a skill that could only have been obtained through the exercise of the most tender sympathies.

This Doctor Witt wore a special cloak, and carried a magicians wand. His skill was said to be great, and his peculiar bearing awakened the respect of all who were at all affected by superstition. He was a magician, and by the stars revealed to his visitors their destiny; he was a conjuror, and relieved the disorders and spells of witchcraft; he was a physician, and healed the diseases of the body, and as he lived for a century, his great age impressed the people with the belief in his special power.

The nearest mills for grinding flour for the settlers in Falkner Swamp were located along the Wissahickon and for a small gift the Indians of their neighborhood would carry on their shoulders the grain, and the next day return with the flour. Their manner of traveling was in single file, each one stepping in the footsteps of their leader. So that Henry Antes was not always alone in his journey, but with such an escort would speed over the hills to the deep vale of the sparkling Wissahickon.

What a wonderful stream the Wissahickon was, as it rolled so tumultuously over its rocky bed, from the great Whitemarsh plain to the broad Schuylkill. Steep were its walls of tree crowned rocks, many were its ravines, and at the foot of each ravine some enterprising settler built his mill to supply the people of the hills above him with the luxuries of life. And here as he journeyed the calculating eye of the young man saw a way to fortune and prosperity.

When Frederick Antes with his family left Germantown, to settle upon the part of the great tract which he had purchased in 1723, there were still retained ties of a social nature stronger far than those which had bound them to the land of their ancestors, and the frequent trips taken from the forest cabin to the town of their kindred revealed to those who dwelt nearer civilization the rapid growth of the youth who with a happy heart and ardent hope called the forest his home. To Christina, the daughter of William Dewees, these visits were occasions of great joy, for she had promised to share the fortunes of life with the brave and noble youth who already was a leader of the people. A merry time was planned by the youth of Germantown to celebrate their marriage. Although in the New World, they would retain their old customs, and as in the districts of old Germany they would here celebrate the marriage, and their festivities would make them feel the more as if they were indeed at home.

With the question of marriage arose several serious considerations. Antes was a thorough churchman, and had been well trained in the customs and laws of the Reformed Church, and although there were many thousands of members of that church in the colony, there was no ordained minister, hence no one duly qualified to administer the ordinance of the church.

What others had done, we do not know, but Antes was too good a Christian to adopt the customs of the wilderness, and too much of a churchman to follow the practices of other religious bodies. And yet his big glowing heart would not be satisfied without the fair Christina. In his perplexity he turned to his friend John Philip Boehm, a man several years older than himself, but one filled with the spirit of the church. Boehm had served as schoolmaster and fore-singer in the city of Worms in the Fatherland, and in 1720 had come across the sea to settle in this growing colony. Many joined with Henry Antes in urging him to assume the labors of a minister until by official authority he could be fully declared to be such by the proper course of vows.

Boehm consented to do so and performed the duties of an ordained minister to the satisfaction of the members of the three Reformed Churches. But in 1727, a regularly ordained minister came and showed the irregularity of this step, and the necessity of having it made right. They appealed to the New York ministers of the Reformed Church, who thought it so grave a matter that it was referred to the Classis of Amsterdam, who upon the petition signed by sixteen officers of the three churches, in 1729, granted their request, declared his acts valid and ordered his ordination.

A proper minister being thus obtained the usual course was followed. Three times in the church at Whitemarsh the banns were published, and the Tuesday following, February 2d, 1726, was selected for the wedding. This was the safe day, it portended no evil forboding. On that day no shadow could rest on the future of the happy couple. It was the day free from jealousies and supernatural visitations. We have no description of the wedding. We may suppose it to have been like this. One of the Old Country marriage observances amongst the better class of people. Early that morning while the stars were yet shining, the active paper manufacturer, William Dewees, had his dwelling prepared for the coming event.

The nearest relatives and a few honored guests partook of the "Morgensuppe" a meal consisting of several dishes of rich viands. As the guests came in, the parents of the bride, attired in their best clothes, welcomed each one with a hearty shake of the hand. Back of them stood the bride with her wreath of rosemary already in her hair. She, too, welcomed the guests, extending her hand to each one, and cheerfully saying to them "Grüss Gott" (God greet thee). To this meal the bridegroom was not admitted.

After this meal, when all are ready for the starting, the best man delivers a speech in which in the name of the bride he thanks the parents for the care, tenderness, love and devotion they have given her. And then the two bridesmaids fasten around the bride's waist the "Ehrengürtel",—a broad leathern girdle plated with silver, and highly ornamented. This girdle meant that the bride had lived a life of purity, was free from all reproach and was well entitled to wear this "girdle of maiden honor." In carriages or on horseback they were to ride to the church, and already at the door the horses were waiting.

The long silky tails and glossy manes of these horses had been braided into numberless little plaits and adorned with red and blue ribbons. The wagons—if such were used—were festooned with wreaths of evergreens from along the Wissahickon.

The friends are ready to give the sending-off shouts and all in silence await the last act at the house. This was the bride feeding the horses that were to take her to church. Laying a slice of bread for each horse on a plate, after besprinkling the former with salt, she steps up to each animal and gives it its share. When she has done this with each one, she walks thrice round the carriage, and after the third time dashes the plate against the right-hand wheel of the vehicle.

They go first to the house where the bridegroom is waiting, here the "best man" lifts the bride to the ground and she enters followed by the party to receive their wedding favors, which are a red and white ribbon knotted around the right arm, while the bridegroom's favors are of violet silk, besides which he wears a bunch of rosemary in his hat.

They now proceed to the church and the ceremony is performed according to the rules of the Reformed Church. After this they return to the home of the bride and partook of the usual wedding dinner—the cabbage dinner—and the company merrily feast on cabbage, with all the savory accompaniments necessary to make it representative of the wealth and liberality of the honorable father of the bride.

How proudly Henry Antes gazed upon Christina as she was given to him to love, cherish, and protect. And beautiful she was with her bright, shining blue eyes, fair skin and flaxen tresses. Her face, round and merry, now wreathed in beams of happiness, for she knew that he in whom she trusted was true, and that the smile of their Heavenly Father rested upon them.

Henry was indeed in youth's ruddy morning, having only passed his twenty-fifty birthday, and was filled with the ambition of youth.

THE WISSAHICKON.

Chapter VII.

The Crefeld Mill, and the Strange People Who Came to It.

WILLIAM DEWEES was undoubtedly a man of most active habits, with a public spirit that led him far in advance of the sober thinking Mennonites who were his fellow citizens in Germantown. We have already seen him as Constable and Sheriff of the morally disposed people, but now we see him in another sphere of usefulness.

In honor of the home across the ocean from which he had come, he named his new enterprise the Crefeld Mills, for at a favorable spot along the Wissahickon he builds a paper and flour mill combined. We do not know whether this was done before the marriage of his daughter to Henry Antes or afterward, for Antes was a millwright, and in these mills was partner with his father-in-law.

Here Antes spent the three years following his wedding, and no place in all the country districts could have afforded better opportunity for him to observe the people who were settling in the land. From all parts of the settlements the people came for their flour, and the learned—and there were many of these—for their paper.

The people of Crefeld who chose the hills above the Wissahickon for their settlement were wise in their choice, and every available spot along that flowing stream was laid hold of to display the industry and business tact which they possessed.

The very wildness of its precipitous banks, the boldness of its rock cliffs and the denseness of its forest growth seemed to add to its general attractiveness, and the steady constant flow of its waters guaranteed a business for every month of the year.

Down its ravines the Indians had made their paths, and these now broadened out into the highways of travel, not such as to admit the dainty carriages of our day, but well suited for the primitive mode of travel adopted by the foot rangers of that day.

The ceaseless rubbing of the mill's great hoppers kept time with the roar and dash of the busy waters, and even the deepening shadows of the early nightfall failed to suppress their energy, and with the falling of the night came the accompanying chorus of thousands of the creatures of forest, swamp, and bush-lined stream. In these hours the thoughtful miller would recall the disturbing and oppressive burdens of the Fatherland, and thank God for the peace of the wilderness. One of the usual scenes that graced the valley in front of the mill was a file of stalwart Indians in silence swiftly trotting along, bearing upon their backs burdens of grain from the distant settlements to be exchanged in these mills for flour.

Henry Antes would be glad to see these troops for they not only brought business, but also news from the many friends in the up country settlements, and well too did he know the nature of their journey, for had he not many times taken this same journey from his father's house to see his beloved in Germantown?

How silently as the evening began to darken the valley, the troop came along, each one stepping in the footprints of the leader, not a word spoken by any of them, only a guttural grunt now and then expressing some conclusion they were welcoming in their thoughts.

On their journeys they were dressed in their gayest attire, for they knew they were a constant source of wonder and admiration to the Germans. On their feet were their soft deerskin moccasins, and leggings, all ornamented according to the wealth of the wearer. Over their huge shoulders were spread skins of wild animals they had killed, that of the bear, or the wolf, while their heads were decorated with the long feathers of the wild turkey, and now and then, one who had been famous in the chase would wear a necklace of bear's claws.

Their copper-colored faces were daubed with

paints of gaudy hues, giving them an expression of fierceness, such as was now held in reserve, for they were friendly with the whites.

Occasionally they murmured at the greed of some settler, or at the encroachment upon their fishing grounds, but they sought peace, and the Germans did not give to them the dreadful "fire-water" which in so many places aroused the children of the forests to deeds of cruelty and blood.

Well they knew the kindly beaming face of the young miller, for by their homes he had set his traps according to their instructions, and had fished in their waters side by side with themselves, and had slept in their huts as one of themselves and they had trusted him.

When their burdens had been cast upon the floor of the mill, was measured, and the equivalent in flour given, they took up their homeward line of march, and only stopped to rest for the night when they came to their usual camping ground in the depths of some thick undergrowth. Then when by themselves, their entire manner was altered. They rapidly talked to each other, smiled and joked, and talked of the impression they had made, and were just as free and easy as even the Germans themselves in their own households. The silence of the Indians was their manner toward strangers, and not their ordinary way of conducting themselves.

But Henry Antes was the happier now, for he had received word from them that his father, mother and sister were well, and the harvests were abundant with the settlers.

Another strange weird group of dwellers in the up country also occasionally passed down the valley to the road winding up through the largest ravine to Germantown. These were the Tunkers, who in numbers of fifty or sixty visited their friends in Germantown.

They walked along in Indian file in a solemn steady pace, keeping straight forward, with their eyes fixed to the ground, not noticing those whom they passed or answering any questions that might be addressed to them. Their dress consisted of a shirt, trowsers, and waistcoat, with a long white gown and cowl of wool in Winter, and linen in Summer. The women in dress differed from the men only in wearing petticoats.

When they went in public they covered their faces with the cowls of their gowns. Their faces were pale and bloodless, for they lived on vegetables solely, and slept on wooden benches, with blocks of wood for pillows.

The sexes dwelt apart, for marriage was forbidden them, and four times a day they attended worship.

William Dewees knew their leaders well, for when they met with persecution in their own land in the county of Witgenstein, they removed to Crefeld in Germany, from whence, under the guidance of Alexander Mack, a miller, they came to Pennsylvania in 1719 and first established themselves in Germantown, and then, some as hermits, some in communities, dispersed to different parts of the wilderness.

But Antes well knew that with all the mortification and maceration of the flesh they practiced, they were far from the ideal state of man, for strife and contention at times waxed fiercely amongst them. With these peculiar people he could find no attractive features. They seemed to belong to the gloom and shade of life, and seemed to be a part of the fleeting evening hour. His own nature was all sunny and bright, sparkling with the beauty of life like the beautiful stream that as a silver thread wound down the narrow rugged valley, yet full of power as here and there it lingered a moment to set in motion the great stones of the various mills.

There was one spot along the creek to which we may suppose the miller often turned his steps. It was a huge rock that stood up high above all its fellows, and above the tallest trees at its base. Back of it stretched the forest along the ridge east of the creek, from its flat top the deep valley for some distance was in view, while the ridge on the other side of the creek was seen stretching away in the distance.

It required expert climbing to reach its summit, but when there, all the grandeur and wildness of the Wissahickon lay before him. It is now called Indian Rock, for the legend is that from its lofty top Indian chiefs were accustomed to addressing their followers who gathered in groups in the valley and under the trees beneath it.

In such a place as this Antes would be likely to meet the hermits, as they loved to seek such places to muse upon the coming of the millenial glory of their Lord. To a mind like Antes' meeting such men in the forest would arouse the greatest curiosity to understand their real views and desires, while meeting an honest, intelligent, enquiring man like Antes they would unfold their thoughts more freely and confidentially than to others. So that we may suppose this period of Antes's life was one of deep reflection upon the peculiarities of human nature and seeing the well-meaning of all these classes, he would be cultivating the desire to bring them all nearer to each other, so that in faith, hope and love they might be one, even as they were one in language.

No reader of this book should suppose that all the Germans were singular people. There were many thousands of Germans, there were but a few of these strange religionists. But so keen is the scent of even historians for the singular and the absurd that they have overlooked the sturdy, quiet thousands to bring out in full particulars the few peculiar ones. Many of these peculiar people were called "Pietists," they were offshoots of the Pietistic movement in Germany.

Kelpius, Pastorius, Falkner, etc., were such, but Antes, Dewees, Boehm and Muhlenberg were church people, and their religious and social customs were ordinary and usual.

These ordinary Germans were our ancestors, let us therefore look at them as being of the most interest to us, for they became the foundation of that part of the State in which they dwelt.

Chapter VIII.

Philadelphia in 1730. The Country M. D.

WHILE Henry Antes was quietly engaged in business on the Wissahickon, the Province was disturbed by several important events.

In June, 1726, Governor Keith reluctantly left his place and was succeeded by Patrick Gordon, a frank, bluff soldier, who kept the loyal anniversaries in a manner quite different from that of the Quakers, and the people celebrated them with him; as, for instance, when the birthday of the Prince of Wales was made a festival at the Governor's house, with drinking of health, salutes of cannon from the decorated shipping, illuminating the house, and even the giving of a ball, which was said to have been the first on record in Philadelphia.

In 1727 disasters seemed to break upon the country in a terrible storm and flood, followed by such a raging sickness that the Assembly could not meet until the regular time for session had gone by.

In 1728 there was a terrible stringency in the money of the Province, riots took place, and the entire Province felt the effects of it, but the authorities granted an increase in the currency, and the danger was partially averted.

In 1730 a great fire on Chestnut street consumed much valuable property.

Antes, now well established at Crefeld, seeing the opportunities for wealth at the rapidly growing settlements, determined to enter again into the frontier life, and began preparations to rejoin his father in Hanover township. But all was not sunshine, and for a while he dreaded removing his wife and three little ones into the dangers of frontier life.

The Indians were mostly peaceful. They were kindly disposed toward the settlers, but all were not saints on either side, and when the bad elements began to work, trouble came.

A settler was killed beyond Conestoga by the Pennsylvania Indians. This aroused fear throughout the settlements, and the Assembly was called on to act in the matter. With firmness and dignity the Assembly demanded of the nation and village to which the criminal belonged his immediate arrest, and threatened if this was not done, to send a force after him, and have him tried by an English jury.

But the greatest danger was from roving bands of non-resident Indians, who in small bands, thoroughly aroused, roved about the settlements, and stimulated by drink and cupidity, committed outrages, destroyed property, stealing the valuables of the settlers, and constantly alarming the females. This became so objectionable that sometimes the bands were driven off by the aroused settlers.

Just at this time, the whole line of settlements in the very part Antes had selected for his habitation, was excited over the raid of such a band. The settlers were called together and they resisted the Indians, a fight ensued and many on both sides were injured, and there was deep apprehension as to the result.

But some of the lawless element took the matter in their own hands. They explored the forests, and coming upon a party of Indians, inhumanly put them to death, and after the deed was committed, discovered that their victims were not of the maurauding party, but belonged to a friendly provincial tribe.

Now indeed there was ground for apprehension, and if the tribes resented this cruel action, death and desolation would speedily devour every frontier settlement

No time was to be lost. The Governor was informed of it, in person he at once proceeded to the spot of the massacre, and there with all the authority of his office commanded the arrest of the murderers, of whom only one escaped.

Still, this did not avert the danger, the chiefs to whom the deceased were related were not reconciled, and it was necessary to call a council, and to secure the arbitration of the chiefs of the Five Nations. Many presents were given, a new treaty was entered into, and the death of each Indian cost the Province a hundred pounds of lawful money.

But peace was again established, and Antes could remove to the settlement with the feeling that there was greater security than before the sad tragedy was enacted.

The settlements quieted down, the swing of the ax once more demanded the laying aside of the musket, and the women went at their work unalarmed by the painted face of a savage foe.

Before leaving Crefeld, Henry Antes availed himself of a privilege which enabled him to be much more useful in life than he could have been if he had neglected it, that was, to become a naturalized citizen of the Kingdom of Great Britain, and a subject of George II.

For the possession of rights and privileges this seemed essential, and although it was rather radical for a German, yet he took the step.

For this purpose he came down to the city of Philadelphia and appeared before the House of Assembly, and there presented his request, and by their formal act was naturalized, and endowed with all the rights before the law, of a citizen.

A trip to Philadelphia at this time was an interesting event. The streets had been laid out in squares, the principal streets at right angles with the Delaware River extending to the Schuylkill.

The population of the city had grown with amazing rapidity, and the spirit of progress was seen on every hand. Benjamin Franklin had just returned from England and was about establishing a newspaper called the Pennsylvania Gazette, and was also making preparations to establish a public library, which he succeeded in doing within a couple of years. Although only about twenty-four years of age, he was rapidly growing into prominence.

Antes must have been interested in the building of the State House, which had now been in progress for about a year. As a mechanic nothing in the city could interest him more. It was to be a great structure, and the pride of the people led them to watch its progress and boast of its magnificence. But as Antes and the people looked upon its walls, as they were being so carefully built, they did not imagine that in forty-six years from that time, within those walls, a paper would be signed by the representatives of the people, which should be the greatest declaration of independence the world ever knew, and from that event, the building should be known all over the world as Independence Hall.

. And little did Henry Antes imagine that in forty-six years from the time he saw the State House being erected, that the result of the Declaration of Independence within its walls by the representatives of every colony of Great Britain in America, would lay the foundation for the grandest of civil governments, and that in the same year and immediately following that declaration in that same building, a convention would meet and draft a constitution for the State of Pennsylvania, and that the young man Benjamin Franklin would be the president of that convention, and Henry Antes' own first-born son, now a little babe of only a few weeks in age, would then be known as Colonel Frederick Antes and as a member from the county of Philadelphia sit with that convention, and vote for the law that no treaty should be made with Great Britain until she should acknowledge the United States should be free and independent, to treat with her in conjunction with the other states concerning peace, amity, and commerce, on just and equal terms.

Having sufficiently observed the workmen, we will imagine Henry Antes sauntering down to Front street, past the mansion of Governor Patrick Gordon, and entering the London Coffee House to refresh himself with dinner. This hotel was the great resort of strangers, and here the events from all parts of the world were first known in the Province, and here German, Englishman, Scotchman, and Quaker sat down to dinner together. The Quakers were the most attractive to Henry Antes, for they were the followers of the great proprietary, and at all times endeavored to carry out the principles of their chief. They were very conservative, and although the following decades presented new phases of social and political life, their principles remained the same, as did also their peculiarities and customs. They were specially noticeable because of their style of dress, which they called plain. They wore clothes of a drab color, or black. High-crowned, broad-brimmed hats be-decked their heads. They always appeared clean shaven, and avoided all jewelry. Their faces generally wore a peaceful expression, and their style of speech was of great tenderness. They sought the most conservative way of expressing themselves, and were careful to speak only after due meditation. In avoiding the pleasures of the world, they also avoided its excesses, and their lives were remarkable for simplicity. They were particularly interested in all things pertaining to the moral elevation of their fellow men, and they bore earnest testimony against all the vices that afflicted their fellow men. They were faithful in all their engagements, and the Indians never had trouble of any kind with them, and any one traveling anywhere in the forests, wearing the Quaker costume, would find protection, relief, and friendship in any Indian's wigwam. In the government of Pennsylvania they had great influence, though as emigrants of a different belief came in, they gradually lost their preponderating power.

Henry Antes, sitting by the window of the London Coffee House, gazed over the river and along the principal street of the city. On every hand he beheld the Quakers, and in the peace and freedom of the Province beheld the effects of their endeavors. How could he feel otherwise than pleased with their spirit and influence. As by his dress and manners they recognized one of the Germans from the town upon the neighboring hill, they treated him kindly, and spoke pleasant words to him. The Quakers respected these German neighbors, for they knew they were men of earnest hearts and pure intentions. They were seeking liberty of conscience and of worship, hence they were brothers. Strange was the speech of the one to the other, but not so the smile, the clasp of the hand, and the tone of the voice.

In strange contrast with the calm, mild mannered Quakers were the fierce eyed Welsh, the boisterous English, the aggressive Scotch-Irish, and the negro—for there were several of these in the Province, and the contrast was exhibited in its most strangely marked features at the water's edge just below the Coffee House, as the small boats brought to the shore the emigrants from the ship that had just arrived. How careful the Quakers were to

settler also purchased a tract to settle upon and farm. But now, he makes the acquaintance of another, who in his community was destined to exert considerable influence. This was John Miller, doctor of medicine.

In those early days the physician was one of the busiest of men. He, like the others, purchased a part of the wilderness, to clear and farm, and at the same time attend to the wants of the people stricken by disease. There were few professional men in those days. Men of culture were not accustomed to brave the perils and fatigues of frontier life. The study of books was denied them, and they could grow only as the wilderness gave them inspiring influences. But these young men, having a desire for learning, boldly determined to develop it though in the face of manifold hindrances, and this they did as the years fled by. The diseases of the settlers were of few types, and these recurred as regularly as the seasons. The cold winds of Winter brought their pneumonias, the floods of Spring their forms of malaria, the heat of Summer and the decay of Autumn their fevers, each one with its hopes brought fears, with its blessings, also its woes. The principles of medicine were few and simple. The lance was carried for blood letting, calomel for malaria, and specifics of great, long hard names which when merely pronounced to the wondering people quieted them into profound awe. Where the opportunities for getting the great medicines became limited, the practical physician turned to his botany and gathered the herbs that grew along every stream, and with teas made of these brought the sick back into health.

The physician's circuit was many miles in diameter, and often he would be away from home for days on his trip. Sometimes fording streams swollen with repeated rains, sometimes following an Indian path for miles through a dense forest, sometimes climbing up mountains so steep that he would be compelled to dismount and lead his horse over the dangers on every hand. Now it would be the fever whose wasting he must check; now, it was consumption that had laid hold of the life of its victim; now, it was some poor fellow who in clearing his land had been struck by a limb of a fallen tree and had been crushed; now, it was the little child too delicate to endure the life of hardship in the comfortless cabin wasting away. To all such the good doctor speedily hurried, and as the minister far away could not come in time, some devout man among the settlers would take his place and administer the consolations of religion.

This labor of love Henry Antes delighted in doing, for at this time the doctor was not a member of the church, though afterward he became one of its elders. What journeys these occasions called forth! The whole community felt the power of their kind deeds! And how this developed character! We can see them as they entered into the borders of the Indian's haunts, going to the remote settlements, carrying blessings and good cheer to all. The Indians wondered at the medicine man and held him in great awe, and to him revealed the marvelous virtues of the plants whose rarity was so marked that uninformed the white man would not have found them. And now we can also see Antes learning the ways of the Indians, studying nature in all her forms, learning the highways in the wilderness, and locating the various tracts already in the market held for sale and of them all carefully searched for the best spot, to purchase for his own home. Dr. John Miller established himself on the public road, and his home became a beacon to the traveler. Every one was supposed to know where he dwelt, and the nearest path to it and hence it was the sign to the travelers as to their road through the land.

THE FIRST MORAVIAN CHURCH IN PHILADELPHIA.

Chapter IX.

The Unitas Fratrum.

THE *Unitas Fratrum*, or The Church of the United Brethren, originated not only in Moravia but also in Bohemia. The blood of the martyr John Huss was its seed. It was founded by some of his followers in 1457 on the Barony of Lititz, in Bohemia. The basis of their union was the following three principles: The Bible is the only source of christian doctrine;. public worship is to be conducted in accordance with the teaching of the Scriptures and on the model of the Apostolic Church; the Lord's Supper is to be received in faith, to be doctrinally defined in the language of the Bible, and every human explanation of that language to be avoided.

Lititz soon became the rallying point for awakened persons throughout Bohemia and Moravia, so that the new church rapidly increased. Its first ministers were priests of the Calixtine or National Church, from which the brethren had seceded. In 1467, however, they introduced a ministry of their own, and secured the episcopacy from Bishop Stephen of the Austrian Waldenses. In spite of frequent persecutions at the hands both of the Roman Catholics and of the National Church, they increased in numbers and influence.

At the beginning of Luther's Reformation in 1518 they had about 200,000 members and over 400 parishes. In the course of time they established colleges and theological seminaries, set up several printing presses, and translated the entire Bible from the original into the Bohemian tongue, which version has remained a standard to the present day. About 1547 they spread to Poland; and in 1557 the *Unitas Fratrum* was divided into three ecclesiastical provinces—the Bohemian, Moravian and Polish, each governed by Bishops of its own, but all united as one church.

Religious liberty having been proclaimed in Bohemia and Moravia in 1609, the Brethren became one of the legally acknowledged churches of these lands. In the early part of the Thirty Years' War, however, Ferdinand II. inaugurated the so-called Anti-Reformation, which crushed evangelical religion out of Bohemia and Moravia. Only a hidden seed of the Church of the Brethren remained. The majority of its members, together with the Lutherans and the Reformed, were driven into exile (1627). A new centre was now established at Lissa in Poland, and many parishes of refugees were formed. But Lissa was destroyed in 1659, in a war between Poland and Sweden, and the remaining parishes were gradually absorbed by other Protestant bodies.

For more than half a century the *Unitas Fratrum* ceased to exist as a visible organization. Its hidden seed in Bohemia and Moravia, however, remained, and its illustrious bishop, Amos Comenius, filled with a prophetical anticipation of its renewal, republished its history, confession and discipline, commended the future Church of the Brethren to the care of the Church of England, and took steps to perpetuate its episcopacy. Hence, for a period of fifty years, clergymen of the Reformed Church were consecrated bishops of the *Unitas Fratrum*, that the succession might not die out. On June 17th, 1722, a few descendents of the Brethren, who had fled from their native land to Saxony, began to build the town of Herrnhut on an estate of Count Zinzendorf, where an asylum had been provided for them. This town soon became the rallying place for the remnant of the Church. descendents of which, to the number of several hundred, immigrated thither from Bohemia and Moravia. They introduced their ancient discipline, handed down by Comenius, and in 1735 received their venerable episcopate at the hands of its two last survivors, Daniel Ernst Jablonsky, and Christian Sitkovins. At the same time, however, many christians from different parts of Germany joined them, so that the renewal of their Church involved a union of the

German element of pietism with the Slavonic element which they represented. The result was a development different from that in Bohemia and Moravia. Count Zinzendorf himself became the leading bishop of the resuscitated Church, and he strove to build it up in such a way as not to interfere with the rights and privileges of the State Church, in the communion of which he had been born, and to which he was sincerely attached. In carrying out this principle he did not let the renewed *Unitas Fratrum* expand as other churches expand, but established on the continent of Europe, in Great Britain, and in America, exclusively Moravian settlements, from which the follies and temptations of the world were excluded, and in which was fostered the highest type of spiritual life." [Bishop E. de Schweinitz.]

Thus in the year 1732 their foreign missionary work began.

Count Zinzendorf also received on his estate other devout refugees with whom the *Unitas Fratrum* maintained the most cordial friendship, among these were the Schwenkfelders, named after their great leader Caspar Schwenkfeld, of Ossing, who was a distinguished teacher at the time of the reformation in the Sixteenth century. His words were of the pure essence of the gospel, mild, tender, and charitable. He appealed to the better instincts of the heart, and sought to instil into the minds of his followers the spiritual walk of Jesus. For nearly two hundred years his followers were tolerated by the German Emperors in Silesia, but in 1590 and 1650 the stroke of persecution fell heavily upon them, and forced to flee they sought protection in Upper Lusatia, in Saxony, under the power of the senate of Gorlitz, and also of Count Zinzendorf; once more forced to flee, they turned their faces toward Pennsylvania. There were not very many of them, but they were distinguished by their industry, frugality, and strict morality, and so greatly were they valued because of these characteristics that in 1742 Frederick of Prussia by special proclamation, invited them to return to their former homes in Silesia.

In looking toward America they first thought of settling in Georgia, when they decided upon Pennsylvania, the lands offered them in Georgia were offered to the Moravians, who accepted the same, and a colony of Moravians in charge of Spangenberg went to Georgia and founded a settlement on the Ogeeche River. This was followed by another colony under Bishop David Nitschman as a preparatory step to a mission among the Creek and Cherokee Indians. Upon the vessel that carried these latter Brethren were General Oglethorpe, John and Charles Wesley, Benjamin Ingram, and Charles Delamotte.

In the year preceding the sending out of these

Moravian colonies, the Schwenkfelders (1734) arrived in Philadelphia, and had with them as their spiritual shepherd George Boenisch, a Moravian, the first Moravian that came into Pennsylvania. After they had been in the colony a year and a quarter George Weiss, one of the Schwenkfelders, was regularly chosen as their spiritual adviser and catechist. This colony was directed to Shippack, halfway between Germantown and the frontier, George Boenish remaining with them for two years, dwelling with Christopher Weigner on the latter's farm. The Schwenkfelders found cordial greeting in Pennsylvania, for, like the Quakers, they were sternly opposed to war, refused to use oaths even in courts of justice, refrained from the use of the sacraments in their religious worship, and in all things sought to possess and manifest the spirit of God.

At this time Henry Antes was in the high tide of business prosperity. He was part owner of the Crefeld Mills, he also owned a plantation in Hanover township, and he was thoroughly interested in securing for the emigrants who were now coming in rapidly, good settlements, at the same time with enthusiastic religious fervor he sought to develop amongst them meetings for praising God. His custom was to call the people together in their houses for singing, prayer, reading the Scriptures, and exhortation. He found no difficulty in affiliating with the Schwenkfelders, and as his associations became the more intimate with them, there were formed many of the sweetest and most enduring friendships of his life. Christopher Weigner's farm became the focal point of the Moravian colonists, and upon it the spirit of God rested as in olden times it rested upon the house of Obed Edom, because the ark of God was there.

The time had now come for Henry Antes to select the place to establish his home. He was in the vigor of manhood, thirty-four years of age, strong, large, and capable of much work. A millwright by trade, a statesman by nature, the friend of all. He was the father of five children, and the duty was impressed on him to look closely after their advantages. Thoroughly acquainted with the country, and with a capital sufficient to enable him to make his choice, he selected a spot as beautiful and advantageous as could be found. The record is "On the second day of September, 1735, Henry Antes of Frederick township, millwright, bought of John Hagerman one hundred and seventy-five acres of land near the branches of the Perkeaming, in Frederick township, paying therefore £200 lawful money of the Province."

Throughout the settlement, each family endeavored to do its own work so far as possible, hence the houses of the people were ordinary log huts, but now and then, some one with more capital would build after the style of the Fatherland. It was a house of this description that Henry Antes erected. The lower story was built of stone, the second story of logs, and this was surmounted by a roomy attic beneath a steep roof. In front of the house on the second story, level with the floor, was a spacious porch, and from this porch could be seen the magnificent valley below them with the smoke curling up in the evenings from neighboring habitations, the far off mountain range bordering the valley, and setting it in a frame of shadowing blue. Since the scenes of ones early life so greatly affect the tone of the mind, the wise builder, by placing his dwelling on this magnificent hill side, conferred a lasting benefit on his children, and the breadth, vigor and beauty of their lifes manifested the results of such influences.

At about the same time Henry Antes entered into partnership with one of the Schwenkfelders, George Hubner, and built a grist mill on the banks of the adjacent creek, and there purchased twenty-eight acres of land adjacent for a better accommodation of their mill. They continued this partnership for nearly twelve years, and then with mutual satisfaction divided their property. This was the first mill of this kind in the settlement, as previous to this all their grain was carried to the mills on the Wissahickon and there exchanged for flour. Antes now supplied the great need, and placed in the mill two pair of stones, under the one roof. When the dissolution of partnership came in 1747, Antes retained the mill, giving Hubner £150 Pennsylvania money and the twenty-eight acres as his share. This article was signed by two faithful men in German. Their names were Abraham Heiderick, the Schwenkfelder, and Adolph Meyer, the Moravian, the latter a "Practitioner in Physick."

Chapter X.

Contemporary Events. German Settlers' Troubles, &c.

IN 1732 the smallpox broke out in Philadelphia and was attended with great fatality. It was difficult to keep even the Assembly in session.

During this time Thomas Penn, one of the sons of the Proprietary, came to Philadelphia, and was received with great pomp and style. The Assembly gave him a banquet; the chiefs of the Five Nations—then visiting Philadelphia—a pow-wow; the fire engines played for him; the freeholders feasted him, and the church wardens and vestry gave him a notable dinner at David Evans' Crown Tavern. The Winter of this year was uncommonly severe, the ice on the Schuylkill being fifteen inches thick, and in the breaking up in Spring there was great damage done, on the Wissahickon as also on the Schuylkill.

In 1733 John Penn, the oldest living son of William Penn, visited the Province and was received in the most elaborate manner, the people turning out en masse to see the sight. The news of what was to be expected had circulated all through the Province. "There was a cavalcade and coach parade, flags flying, and guns firing on Society Hill and from the ships in the river." There were addresses, banquets, and salutes in abundance. While at the height Michael Welfare, one of the Conestoga hermits, appeared in his linen pilgrim's garb, with his tall staff and long venerable beard, standing in the market-place, announcing the judgments of an offended Deity against the iniquitous place. For a quarter of an hour he railed at the crowd and then returned to his Patmos above the Wissahickon."

"In 1736 there was a great treaty made with the chiefs of the Six Nations. The council was held in the Quaker Meeting-house, corner of Second and Market streets, in September and October, under the appropriate auspices of James Logan. One hundred of the chiefs were present, and Logan entertained them for three days at Stenton before the council. At the Meeting-house the chiefs sat in the body of the house, the galleries crowded with spectators. The Seneca chief Kanickhungo, was the principal speaker, and the subject of the conference was the continuance of peace and friendship. Many presents were exchanged, and the conference gathered solemnity from the certainty in the minds of all that an Indian war was not far distant." Such an event would certainly be known to all the Indians of the Province, and be looked to with the most intense interest, and to the settlers also, particularly the Germans who were so rapidly seeking the frontier.

During this period, Antes, as a leading man, was deeply interested in the treatment of the Germans along the Susquehanna, and the borders of Maryland. The uncertainty of the State boundaries increased the trouble. "Many of the Palatines had settled west of the Susquehanna (York Co.) under Pennsylvania titles, but in order to avoid the payment of taxes imposed by the Province, they accepted titles from Maryland, and attorned to Lord Baltimore; but becoming satisfied that adhesion to him might ultimately prejudice their interests, they formally renounced their allegiance, and sought protection from Pennsylvania. This tergiversation irritated the Maryland authorities, and the Sheriff of Baltimore County with three hundred men marched to eject the Palatines from their possessions." This led to many contests, some lives were lost, the border was made unsafe, the Germans were harassed perpetually, and many driven from their farms. This continued until August 1737 when the order was promulgated "requiring the governors of the respective provinces effectually to check the disturbances on the borders, and to refrain from granting lands in dispute, even in the territories, until the king's pleasure should be further known.

Another trouble at this time were the claims of the settlers for their lands. "The proprietary land office had been closed from the year 1718 to the year 1732, during the minorities of Richard and Thomas Penn; and warrants and patents, the usual muniments of title, were not issued by the commissioners of property, but tickets signed by one of the commissioners, or by the secretary of the land office were substituted. Immigrants seated themselves without title, and in many instances without a ticket, upon such vacant lands as they found convenient. The number of settlers of this kind entitled them to great consideration. Their rights, accruing by priority of settlement, were recognized by the public and passed with their improvements, through many hands, in confidence, that they would receive the proprietary sanction. And the practice of the land office, when opened, giving preference to actual settlers, confirmed this expectation. Great agitation was therefore produced by a proprietary proclamation of November, 1738, requiring this class of settlers, and those who had obtained warrants, but had not paid for them, before the first of March next ensuing, to pay to the receiver-general the sums due for their lands under the penalty of ejectment." This caused considerable anxiety among the settlers, threats were made, but as the authorities were not able to carry them out, many compromises were made. These things give us a picture of border worriments, the subject of conversation at their firesides, the eager search for information as to the course of events from such men as Antes, and the incentives to frequent trips from the settlements into the city. It also shows us how a certain degree of mistrust grew up between the Germans and the English, which was deepened by their ignorance of each others language and laws. As an adviser to the ignorant settlers Henry Antes rendered incalculable benefit, for they trusted his integrity and judgment.

CHAPTER XI.

Spangenberg and Whitefield.

GEORGE BOENISCH was a faithful pioneer of the Moravian faith, and his influence was felt throughout the new settlement, but the time had now come for one of the leaders of the *Unitas Fratrum* to enter and reap the harvest. Accordingly in March, 1736, Bishop Spangenberg was instructed to leave the work in Georgia, and proceed to the settlement in Pennsylvania, and there take charge of the work begun by Boenisch. Spangenberg spent three months at St. Thomas, and four months in Georgia, and then proceeded to Pennsylvania.

About the time of the Bishop's coming, Antes recorded in his family Bible " 5th October, 1736, a son was born to me this morning at three o'clock. I named him John Henry! The Saviour preserve him to eternal life. He was baptised by John Philip Boehm. I myself stood as sponsor at the baptism."

Bishop Spangenberg labored with these people until recalled to Europe in 1739. He was the right man to build up the cause he had at heart. Fitted by nature, education, and a peculiarly winning grace to draw out and deepen the spirituality of those with whom he associated. His age was about the same as that of Antes,—only a couple of years past thirty. He was just in his prime, with all the enthusiasm of a brave young man. When only twenty-two years of age he graduated at Jena and at twenty-seven became professor at the University of Halle, and assistant superintendent of Franke's Orphan House, but, two years later, in 1733, because of his too liberal views on church fellowship, he was dismissed, and he then joined the Moravians. Count Zinzendorf appreciating his gifts and graces appointed him as his assistant, sent him to Georgia to locate the Moravian settlement there, and thence to proceed to Pennsylvania to do missionary work among the settlers. His spirit is well shown in a story of one of his experiences in the wilderness when visiting the Onondaga Indians in company with David Zeisberger the great Indian missionary. "One day, all means of subsistence in the forests failed the pilgrims. They were exhausted by hunger and fatigue. Spangenberg turned to Zeisberger, and said affectionately, ' My dear David, get your fishing tackle ready, and catch us a mess of fish.' The other declined, since there could be no fish in such clear water, especially at that time of year. Spangenberg said, ' Inasmuch as I ask it, my dear David, fish! Do it this once, if only out of obedience.' ' Well, I will do it,' he said, but thought in his heart, 'The dear brother knows just nothing about fish; and, indeed, it is out of his line of business.' But when he cast his net, how was he surprised at once to find it full of a multitude of great fishes! The hungry men not only supplied their hunger, but by drying the rest at the fire made quite a provision for their further journey. 'Did I not say to thee,' Spangenberg asked with a smile 'that we have a good Heavenly Father?'"

With that same faith in success and dependence on God, Spangenberg enters upon his work with the Schwenkfelders. Those who attended the meetings, which were now held regularly on Sundays at the house of Christopher Weigner, formed an association which they called "The Associated Brethren of Skippack," among whom are mentioned Henry Frey, John Kooker, George Merkel, Christian Weber, John Bonn, Jacob Wenzen, Jost Schmidt, William Bossen, and Jost Becker, of Skippack; Henry Antes, William Frey, George Stiefel, Henry Holstein, and Andrew Frey, of Frederick; Matthias Gehmelen, and Abraham Wagner, of Matetsche; John Bertolet, Francis Ritter, and William Pott, of Oley; John Bechtel, John A. Gruber, Blasius Mackinet, and George Bensel, of Germantown. In addition to their weekly meetings, monthly conferences were held in which the religious condition of the Germans in the Province was discussed, and certain members appointed to special fields for labor. Bishop Spangenberg and Weigner were selected for Skippack; John Bechtel and John A. Gruber, for Germantown, and Henry Antes, Andrew Frey and George Stiefel for Frederick. These conferences continued until 1740.

It was during this period of earnest religious work that death entered into Antes' household, and took on June 6th, 1739, their nine-month's-old baby Jacob. The first grave they made in the wilderness was that of their youngest.

During this same period, in 1738, when the influence of Spangenberg was arousing all the ardor of these religious people, Gruber issued an address in which he suggested a union of the various sects among the Germans of Pennsylvania. One writer described that time as being "a complete Babel of sects."

As there were between thirty and forty thousand Germans in the colony, and immigration was continuing multitudinously, the desire for union was in the truest sense devout and patriotic. This idea took firm possession of Antes' mind, and became the aim of his life. Rev. John Bechtel afterward wrote of this period "The Sainted Brother Antes, Stiefel, Adam Gruber, myself and others from Germantown, enjoyed many blessed hours together." And who can doubt but that much of their enjoyment came from the exquisite delight in this aim, an aim which to-day urges the greatest of the world's

Evangelists on in their work, and has caused the production of a blessed literature from the pens of such men as Dwight Moody, Bishop Coxe, Washington Gladden, A. J. Gordon and others. But of all those who in that early day aimed at this noble unity, Henry Antes was the most ardent, consistent and persistent, and when failure came down upon it with its mountain bulk and weight of prejudice, Antes felt that there was no more for him to do amongst his fellows, and yielded his spirit to the sovereign of all.

This noble endeavor was not to proceed in the peaceful spirit its advocates hoped, for, although it disclaimed any interference with the ecclesiastical ties of its advocates, it awakened suspicion and antagonism of a very unpleasant character, and this Antes felt severely. Up to the beginning of the year 1740 he continued his membership in the Falkner Swamp Reformed Church, of which Rev. John Philip Boehm was the pastor. But as the religious work grew under the labors of these laymen, the influence of the church seemed to be lost upon them, and many times Antes and his pastor had unpleasant meetings with each other, until at length there was a rupture of pastoral and social relations between them. About this time, on March 13th, 1740, another son was added to Antes' household. He named him John, and recorded the prayer "that the Dear Savior preserve him to eternal life." This son became a great Moravian missionary, and lived a truly consecrated life. Boehm was no longer his beloved pastor, and his now nearer and dearer friend Bishop Spangenberg baptized the child. But a friendship of twenty years' standing cannot be severed without deep sorrow, particularly by so large-hearted a man as Henry Antes.

Bishop Spangenberg now returned to Europe, and his place was taken by Andrew Eschenbach, from Naumberg, who was sent by the Moravian Church to America to continue the work, and to look after the spiritual welfare of the German immigrants scattered throughout the four counties of the Province. This noble man sought his work as soon as the ship arrived in Philadelphia and at once coming to the populous district of Oley—where Antes had been teaching since 1736—made this the central point of his gospel ministry, and for more than two years labored with untiring industry, persuasive eloquence, and decided success.

This same year the Moravians were reinforced by the arrival of those who had perilously gone to Georgia to establish a settlement there. The story of the settlement of Georgia is of thrilling interest. The hopes of the few Moravians who accompanied Bishop Spangenberg there in 1735 seemed to be well founded, but, unfortunately the Spaniards possessed Florida. The boundaries of the States was a question in dispute, which could only be settled by war, and when this came the Moravians saw the hopelessness of their cause, and during the year 1740 abandoned their undertaking and sailed to Pennsylvania. Homes and employment were given to many of them in Germantown, while the others found hearty welcome, and watch-care at Christopher Weigner's.

During this year another event occurred which was a strong link in the chain of events moulding the life of Antes. That was the visit of George Whitefield to Pennsylvania. Mr. William Seward, who accompanied him, makes the follow entry in his diary, "April 24th, 1740, Came to Christopher Weigner's plantation in Skippack, where many Dutch people are settled, and where the famous Mr. Spangenberg resided lately. It was surprising to see such a multitude of people gathered together in such a wilderness country thirty miles from Philadelphia.   *   *   Our dear friend Peter Bohler preached in Dutch, to those who could not understand our Brother Whitefield in English.—Came to Henry Antes' plantation in Frederick township, ten miles further in the country, where was also a multitude equally surprising with that we had in the morning.   *   *   There was much melting under both sermons.   *   *
At night I was drawn to sing and pray with our brethren in the fields. Brother Whitefield was very weak in body, but the Lord Jehovah was his

strength * * for I never heard him speak more clear and powerful. They were German where we dined and supp'd, and they play'd and sung in Dutch, as we did in English, before and after eating. April 25th, rose at three o'clock, and rode near fifty miles to Amwell."

What a wonderful scene that was, when Whitefield stood on Antes' porch and preached to an audience of two thousand people, the religious settlers of the wilderness. No wonder that he preached with unwonted power and enthusiasm, for this great German audience first made the land ring with the melody of their hymns. They were used to singing in the open air and all sung, and such a scene, in which there was an entire absence of affectation, and the presence of the spirit in power, seldom greeted the great preacher. It was in Spring. The electric power of such harmony quickly leaped from soul to soul! Whitefield was in his prime. He was only twenty-six years of age, and had been preaching four years, being everywhere greeted by immense throngs of people who readily yielded to his overwhelming influence. Even the people whom the great Wesley failed to stir could not resist the power of Whitefield. On the vessel that brought him to America the sailors had been persuaded that he was an impostor, but he won them by his magic eloquence, and twice a day expounded to them the Scriptures. He was antagonized by the regular ministry, for his ways were not the stereotyped ways of the schools. Although an Oxfordian, his learning was not great, but he had the peculiar gift of saying just the thing that would touch the hearts of the people.

With a thoroughly generous spirit, he felt the needs of orphans, and in connection with his preaching collected money to establish an orphan asylum in Georgia, and also seeing the need of the colored people, desired to establish a school for their education. His coming to Pennsylvania caused the most intense feeling amongst friends and foes. Gordon in his history of Pennsylvania says:—" The year 1740 is remarkable in the annals of Pennsylvania for the labors of the celebrated, enthusiastic, itinerant Whitefield. He landed at Lewistown in November, 1739, and soon after came to Philadelphia. His arrival disturbed the religious harmony which had prevailed since the time of Keith. He drew to himself many followers from all denominations, who influenced by the energy of his manner, the thunder of his voice, and his flowing eloquence, were ready to subscribe his unnatural and incomprehensible faith, professing their willingness to endure eternal damnation, that they might be forever saved. His disciples were chiefly the illiterate and uninformed, who made up in zeal what they lacked in knowledge. Like most reformers he turned the force of his artillery against the amusements and pleasures of society. His attendant, Seward, announced in the Gazette, that since Mr. Whitefield's preaching, the dancing school, assembly, and concert room had been closed, as inconsistent with the doctrines of the Gospel; and though the gentlemen concerned had broken open the doors, no company attended on their invitation." Evidently Mr. Gordon was not a friend to religion among the masses, though he must record the wonderful influence of the preacher.

Benjamin Franklin was a friend to the great preacher, and Franklin was a clear headed philosopher who would not have given his approval to a man who could only move the illiterate. Of Franklin it is said that on one occasion he heard Whitefield pleading for his Orphan House. At first he decided that he would not give anything, but as the speaker proceeded, he concluded he would give a small amount, but when the speaker had finished his appeal, unable to resist, Franklin emptied the entire contents of his purse on the plate. Whitefield's voice was marvelous. It was said to be an organ, a flute, a harp all in one, and that he was able to produce every emotion of the human heart by pronouncing the word "Mesopotamia." "Dr. Lathrop related a scene which he had witnessed, without any feeling, to Mr. Whitefield. The same day, Dr. Lathrop listened to the same story, by Mr. Whitefield, and found himself bathed in tears."

Such was the fearless, eloquent, godly man who in an unknown tongue spake to the Germans of Pennsylvania. How much Antes understood we do not know, but it is very probable that he was acquainted with the English language, and from this time on he became Whitefield's friend and helper in the work. With a heart already on fire for the work of the Lord, the influence of the great preacher added to its intensity until its heat and light flamed forth on every side.

With such men there was no time for delay, every hour was precious, life was too short to spend any of it in loitering, hence, though this meeting had been very precious, and the whole country was stirred, they must at once proceed on their way. We have already noted that at three o'clock the next morning the preacher and his party were on their way, with a long journey before them, but at that time another party set forward. Whitefield was filled with the desire of establishing a school for negroes. For this purpose he had purchased a tract of 5000 acres of land in the Forks of the Delaware, upon which, in a suitable place the school could be built. Now he thinks he has found the proper men to do this work for him. Thus we see that Antes made a strikingly favorable impression upon the great evangelist. Bohler and Seyffert of the Moravians, with Henry Antes as their guide, started to view the purchase, and arrange for the beginning of the school. They travelled all day. How sweet their conversation must have been as they rode their horses through the unbroken forest and recalled the tone, the manner, the fiery glance, the impassioned appeal, and the glowing words of the evangelist the day before. At length they arrived at an extensive Indian village, in the beautiful valley of the Forks, and there in the woods spent the hours of the night. The next day they examined the property. The Indians were friendly —possibly they were known by Antes, who now serving as guide must have before been along these forest paths. They decided on the spot to locate the school, and then returned to Antes' home. It was then decided that Bohler should superintend the work, while several who were good mechanics would do the work. Antes and Seyffert, both good mechanics, thoroughly supported Bohler in the plans agreed upon.

On the 19th of May, 1740, fourteen persons, Bohler, Antes, Seyffert, seven Moravian brethren, two sisters and two boys who had come from Georgia the preceding April, arrived at the Indian village, and began the erection of a building on a spot which from that day to this is known as Nazareth. But as often happens, the work was retarded. Before the building was completed the ardent philanthropist and evangelist was thrown into financial embarrassment, and compelled to relinquish his worthy project, but the ideas of these Germans had been fastened on this work, and in Antes' hands, although in a slightly different way, the plans of the evangelist were destined to be carried to a successful completion.

Chapter XII.

The Founding of Bethlehem.

"1741 was an unhappy year for Philadelphia—discontent, wars, rumors of wars, pestilence, famine and distress among the poor, dissensions among those in power and place. The currency was disordered, the home government and the city people differing about the rates to be paid for foreign coins. There were large fires—the Governor's mills on the Cohocksink, and Hamilton's building on the river front, being burnt. The severe weather of the Winter caused so much distress among the poor that the regular resources were exhausted, and the Common Council had to make an additional appropriation and appoint a committee to solicit subscriptions for relief. There were riots (growing out of the scarcity of small change), so that the Common Council had to establish a rallying signal for the citizens to rendezvous at central points for the suppression of outbreaks, and order a sort of curfew to compel negroes to go home early and cease their riotous assemblages. There was a serious epidemic outbreak of yellow fever, the cause of which was either West Indies importation or the bad condition of the dock. The Governor and Assembly had a quarrel about it, and the result was a heavy increase of mortality. There were seven hundred and eighty-five burials during the year, an increase of five hundred and five over the preceding year. The disease was called the Palatine fever, and two hundred and six of these immigrants fell victims to it. But it caused a thorough examination of the condition of the quarantine, and a remedy for the troubles. It is sad to reflect that this terrible state of affairs had resulted from the quarrels between the Quakers and the Governor's party, and the refusal of the Assembly to pay the quarantine physician for his services.

It may not be amiss at this point to notice the general political condition of the Province. In the city of Philadelphia there were two parties which were showing their antagonism in every possible form, and bringing all questions in dispute. The one party was headed by the Governor, who had associated with the aristocracy, from a political point of view. As usual with that class, the love of pomp and power prevailed over principle. The other party was under the control of the Friends' Meeting, and was largely made up of the Quakers with others who desired the ways of peace. During the Spanish war, the enemy had kept several privateers along the coast, which sadly interfered with the colonial commerce. The Governor recommended the Assembly to equip vessels of war, to grant a bounty for every enemy killed or taken, and to provide for the families of seamen killed or wounded in the service, but the Assembly in a characteristic spirit resolved, that if the royal navy at Boston, New York, and in Virginia, were inadequate for the protection of the coast, little could be expected from them, situated so remotely from the sea, and unable to sustain the expense.

This same war, now located in the West Indies occasioned great demands by friend and foe for provisions. To prevent the supply of the enemy an embargo was laid on all sorts of provisions in Great Britain and Ireland, and a bill interdicting their export, except to the British dominions, was introduced into Parliament. But the zeal of Governor Thomas had anticipated this measure in Pennsylvania, by proclamation, limiting the export of provisions to British ports. He endeavored to prevail on the Assembly to entirely prohibit the export of wheat. The House not only refused his request, but intimated that he was fortunately protected by the King's proclamation and act of Parliament from an inquiry into the legality of the restriction which he had himself laid upon commerce.

The crowded state of the passenger ships from Ireland and Germany, sometimes engendering pestilential fevers, had early invited the attention of the Legislature. The landing of infected passengers in the city was forbidden; but ample provision was not made for the sickly emigrants. Governor Thomas had frequently recommended to the Assembly to build a lazaretto, but they had hitherto pleaded their poverty. Dr. Graeme, the port physician, whose duty it was to visit all unhealthy vessels, having resigned his office, in consequence of the refusal of the Assembly to pay his account, was succeeded by Dr. Zacharry Lloyd, by the appointment of the Assembly. A virulent dispute was engendered by the Governor's denial of the right of the House to appoint this officer; and, during the contest, the duties of the place being neglected, a contagious distemper, attended by great mortality, was introduced into the city, from some vessels having German passengers on board. This afflicting dispensation was charitably ascribed by the Governor and Assembly each to the other, by having suspended or impeded the duties of the port physician. Both parties made the dispute a means for flattering the Germans, whom they proclaimed to be an honest and valuable portion of the population. All fears of foreigners had faded away; and each charged the other with the hostility which both had displayed against foreigners generally. The Germans now formed a large proportion of the landholders of the Province; and, what was at present more to the purpose, a large proportion of the voters, who must determine the character of the next Assembly.

From this dispute grew the determination of the House to establish a lazaretto. An island, subsequently called Providence Island, a valuable tract of three hundred and forty-two acres, situated at the confluence of the rivers Delaware and Schuylkill, was purchased. The property was vested in trustees who were created a board of health, with the necessary power to prevent the approach of sickly vessels to the town, and to retain diseased passengers until convalescent. The expense incurred was chargeable on the importer, to whom recourse was given against the effects of the passengers. The quarrel between the Governor and Assembly became uncontrollable, either by official forms or a sense of public decorum. Charges of untruth, imposture, hypocrisy, tyranny, and faction, disgraced the addresses of the one and the replies of the other. The Governor, having lost all hope of convincing the House, or reforming its conduct, wrote messages only to open the eyes of its deluded constituents; while the House charged him with the design of subverting the liberties of the people. They found evidence in support of this allegation in his correspondence with the ministry, copies of which had been procured and transmitted by the Provincial agent. To obtain favor with the Crown, and to protect himself against the remonstrance of the Assembly, the Governor had represented it as vain to hope for military aid from Pennsylvania, whilst the Quakers had the right of sitting in the Assembly, and that body was empowered to dispose of public money, and to meet and adjourn at pleasure. These privileges, he earnestly recommended should be suppressed. He represented, that the Quakers, by the direction of the Yearly Meeting, had been unusually active in procuring seats in the Assembly; and that of thirty members, three only were not of that sect. That they had abused the confidence of the Germans; had predjudiced them against the Government, by inducing them to believe that a mild militia law would reduce them to slavery, such as they had suffered under the German princes; that they would be impoverished by the expense, would be dragged from their farms, and compelled to build forts, in return for their admission into the Province. He stated the Province to be rapidly increasing in population, and its wealth to be £10,000 in bank, and an annual income of £7500, from the loan office and excise. He portrayed the conduct of the Assembly in the darkest colors, and expressed a wish to resign as soon as he could safely transport himself and family to England.

When the time for the elections came, the streets of Philadelphia became the arena of rioting and bloodshed. Sailors from the vessels in the river came upon the people and attacked them with clubs, but the country people rallied to the defence of their privileges and drove the sailors back to their ships. The Quakers were supported by the Germans, and the Governor's party was defeated. While this was going on in Philadelphia Henry Antes was laboring in the German settlements to establish harmony, righteousness and peace among the people, and yet, such is the false view of popular historians that his name has been overlooked in the pages of history while attention has centered on the doings of unscrupulous agitators and politicians.

The work by the ardent Eschenbach was also growing, and Evangelical truth was flourishing all through that part of the Province. It was a battle of true religion against men, form, and meaningless pretention. At this time Antes was still a member of the Reformed Church, but the boon companion of the Moravian missionaries, and as we have seen the ally of Whitefield. The religious movement was bitterly opposed by denominationalism. From that stand-point the dearth of religion was dreadful. For instance, from the Lutherian point of view it is thus described,—"His (Henry M. Muhlenberg, the first Lutheran minister in 1742) coming was most opportune. There were none to minister to the religious wants of the people, except several self-constituted pastors, who were men without education and without piety. Though the first Germans n America were men of earnest devotions, they could not, without religious advisers, retain their piety, or transmit it to their children. They consequently declined rapidly in spirituality. When Muhlenberg came he found their religious condition deplorable. There were no churches and no schoolhouses, save one building in New Hanover, and that too poor for occupancy. He at once undertook to build churches and schoolhouses for the religious and secular instruction of both old and young. Very few of the young could read, and teachers of suitable character and qualifications could not be procured. So Muhlenberg became both pastor and teacher. "Necessity," he says, "has compelled me to become a teacher of the children. One week I keep school in Philadelphia, the next in Providence, and the third in New Hanover; and I think God's grace is visiting us. It was, however, high time that I should come. If affairs had remained a few years longer in the same state in which I found them, our poor Lutherans would have been scattered or turned over to heathenism."

Describing the religious condition of the country, he says, "Atheists, deists, and naturalists are to be met with everywhere. I think there is not a sect in the Christian world that has not followers here. You meet with persons from almost every nation in the world. God and his Word are openly blasphemed. Here are thousands who by birth, education and confirmation, ought to belong to our church, but they are scattered to the four winds of heaven. The spiritual state of our people is so wretched as to cause us to shed tears in abundance. The young people are grown up without education and without the knowledge of religion, and are turning to heathenism." Muhlenberg was a thoroughly evangelical preacher, and became a power for good in the land, but he was thoroughly denominational, and looked at things in the light of Lutheran Church interests largely.

On the part of the Reformed was Michael Schlatter, whose biography gives this account: "The original emigration from Germany, which forms the root of the two denominations in America known as the Reformed and the Lutherans, came from that province in Germany then known as the Palatinate. It is the most fertile and the most beautiful part of Germany, lying on its frontiers over against France, through which contending armies have for ages passed and repassed. It has long since ceased to be a separate kingdom. A portion of it (Rhenish Bavaria) belongs now to Bavaria; another portion, with the ancient capital Heidleberg, forms the southern part of Baden; and a third portion has recently been annexed to Prussia. At this time (1730) the Reformed, holding to the old Reformed confession, constitute more than one-half of the whole number of the German emigrants to Pennsylvania, being about 15,000. These Germans formed in many instances the outposts of civilization, and served to protect not a few English

THE FIRST REFORMED CHURCH IN PHILAD'A

communities from the incursions of the Indians. But the people were mostly poor. They were not able to bring ministers of the gospel with them, but they brought over their Bibles, catechisms, hymn books, and devotional works. In many settlements they had pious and excellent schoolmasters. In most cases they formed congregations, built churches and by their side at once planted school-houses, each with a dwelling and land for the occupancy of the schoolmaster. These often, when there was no minister, conducted a religious service by the reading of sermons and prayers, and the people sought and found spiritual edification in these services, and in singing the grand old hymns and chorals of the Fatherland. As early as 1726 a log church was built in Skippack, Pennsylvania. A few ministers came from Germany, and extended their labors with considerable success over the various German settlements. The man who was to organize these congregations into a compact whole, and thus to lay a stable foundation for future growth, was the Rev. Michael Schlatter."

The Reformed view was more encouraging than the Lutheran, but in the prosecution of evangelistic work by the Moravians, both united in opposition, seeing no good in it. John Philip Boehm, the pastor of the Reformed Church, was like Muhlenberg and Schlatter, a brave, zealous, hard working pastor, but thoroughly denominational. He was quite a missionary pastor, and had congregations in Philadelphia, Germantown, Whitpain, Forks of the Delaware, Hanover, Skippack and Whitemarsh, and in addition was quite a land owner. He was a man of ability, a fine penman, and a careful preserver of all records pertaining to his church. But with all his excellence, he was far inferior to Antes in breadth of view, and, incapable of realizing the greatness of the idea that controlled Antes, set his face against it, and with voice, pen, and personal influence, sought to prevent it from being consummated. Muhlenberg, when he came, joined with him, and thus denominationalism sought to destroy the purest form of evangelicalism. Perhaps it did not seem so to them, but to-day we can see how far Antes was superior to his time, for now the noblest souls of our denominations are hoping and praying for just such a union as he aimed at, and to-day we see clearly that one of the greatest, if not the greatest of foes to the spread of the truth of Christ and success in mission work, is that same spirit of denominationalism.

Antes loved the Reformed communion, but he loved souls better, and his brave heart would not be turned from the course it had marked out to develop the Master's Kingdom. There now came another of the bishops of the Moravian Church, David Nitchman, who had formerly been with them, but had returned to Europe. There also came another prominent worker, David Zeisberger, Sr. These men came to consult with Henry Antes in regard to a suitable place for establishing a Moravian settlement. For this purpose they had received various offers, such as a place in Frederick, and a place in New Hanover, but their attention was directed to the plans of Whitefield, in the Forks of the Delaware, which had failed, leaving there a colony of brave hearted Moravians. Henry Antes for and in behalf of the Moravian Brethren, purchased of William Allen for £400, five hundred acres located on Monacacy Creek and the west branch of the Delaware River, now known as the Lehigh. It is upon this ground the city of Bethlehem now stands, and this became the first peculiarly Moravian settlement in Pennsylvania.

Chapter XIII.

Zinzendorf and the Conferences.

ON the 10th day of December, 1741, there appeared on the scene a new character to aid in moulding the features of the times. This was Nicholas Lewis, Count of Zinzendorf and Pottendorf, but familiarly known as Count Zinzendorf. Of all the men who visited the Province there was no one superior to this great man. At this time he was forty-one years of age, of middle stature, inclining toward corpulency, with a countenance glowing with a holy light, which was shed from his dark brown eyes over all his features. In his bearing there was a hearty affability joined with noble manners, and priestly devotion. One has written of him, "Zinzendorf, as had been his wont for many years, spent the entire afternoon, (Sunday) in retirement, communing with God respecting himself and the plans for the church under his care. That blessed look, often seen in him when he was in the spirit on the Lord's day, attracted those nearest him to go close to him, not to address him, which they carefully avoided, but simply to cast a glance upon him. The last Sundays of his life his eyes had more than once been seen full of tears, giving them such a blessed expression as impressed deeply the hearts of his most attached friends."

No doubt but that from Spangenberg, Nitchman and Eschenbach, Antes had often heard of this noble bishop, and had longed to behold him, and no doubt but that the Count had heard of Antes, the bold soldier of the Lord in the wilderness, and the helper of his people, so that when the opportunity came, they lost no time in becoming acquainted, and in communing with each other in regard to the one work which they both cherished within their hearts.

But that we may the better appreciate this noble character, let us look at his life, for he was one of the Lord's own, called in answer to prayer, for a special purpose, to do a needed work. "His father, a christian statesman and court minister of electoral Saxony, had taken part with Spener, and had received from him, when forming a second marriage with the Baroness Von Gersdorf, his wishes that they might be given a pious posterity and godly wisdom, by which to save them from the prevailing degeneracy. 'For,' said Spener, 'in these corrupt times it seems to men almost impossible to bring up children, of the higher rank, especially, as christians.' Nicholas was the only child of this marriage. Spener was his god-parent, along with the electoral princesses of Saxony, and of the Palatinate. In a

visit, shortly before the close of his life, Spener laid his hands on the boy of four years and gave him his blessing." Zinzendorf himself has said, "My dear grandmother kept me for ten years in her own chamber, my Aunt Henrietta prayed with me morning and evening, and passed the day in accord with the prayer. In my fourth year I began to seek God with such earnestness as accorded with my childish notions. From that time especially, it was my steadfast resolve to become a true servant of the crucified Jesus. The first profound impression upon my heart was made by what my mother told me of my blessed father, and of his hearty love for the martyred person of the Savior. * *
I recollect weeping once very bitterly because, in family worship, I lost, by falling asleep, the verse, 'Thou art our dear father, because Christ is our dear brother.' This thought sweetly impressed me in my fourth or fifth year, for I believed that as soon as one was pardoned, he was in the company of the Savior as a brother.'"

"At this time of his childhood Zinzendorf wrote tender letters to the Savior, and threw them out of the window, confident that the Lord would receive them and read them." "Very early this heart was tried by deep-reaching speculations. 'In my eighth year,' he says, 'I was led by a song which my grandmother sang at bedtime into a revery and profound speculation which kept me awake the whole night, and made me unconscious of hearing or seeing. The most subtle atheistic notions entered my mind. I was so wrought upon by them, and so prostrated, that all which I have read and heard since of unbelieving doubts prove very shallow and weak, and make no impression upon me.' By the use of his will, the boy forever subdued this assault. 'What I fancied that grew odious to me, what I believed, that I willed,' he says, 'I resolved at once to use my understanding in earthly things whenever necessity arose, and to brighten and to sharpen it, since by it only could progress be made; but in spiritual things to abide simply by the truth apprehended in the heart, making this the foundation for the acquirement of truth. What I could not bring in connection therewith I resolved to cast utterly away.' Thus Zinzendorf's theology became, in accordance with its origin, a heart theology. It was free from all refinements respecting the foundations and the abysses of existence. It aimed with its entire strength at Christian living and doing. This it was which gave it its limitation but also power."

When ten years of age Zinzendorf was sent to Halle, then under the charge of Francke. Many of the Pietists were associated there, and the devout boy found it one of the most delightful experiences of his life. The nature of his life's work was there manifested, in his forming associations with friends of like spirit. With Frederick of Watteville, Zinzendorf made an especial compact for the conversion of the heathen, and of those especially to whom no one else would go. Thus, as it often occurs in life, school-life became a prophecy of the after career. When sixteen years of age he was sent to Wittenberg to fit him for an honorable career in the service of the state, and to tone down his religious zeal, but this not succeeding, when nineteen, he was removed to Utrecht. "Here he read law, theology, acquired English, and entered into the theological controversies with the reformed and with the doctors of philosophy, and soon found out that his reasonings were insufficient. After a while he continued his travels to Paris, which was the resort of other young German nobles for the sake of the excitements of the luxurious city, and the pleasures of its court. Zinzendorf not only lived with thoroughly pure morals, but sought the acquaintance of earnest Christians among the priests and bishops of the Catholic communion, and indeed became quite intimate with the devout Archbishop of Paris, Cardinal Noailles.

He found the prelates as firmly established in their church belief as he was in his. They soon agreed on both sides to lay aside controversy in order to join in the love of Christ. In 1738 he wrote, 'Moreover, I cherish and highly esteem, according to my way, all who love Jesus. I would consider myself very unhappy to be counted an alien by any Catholic who loves Christ, although in many points I differ wholly from their opinions.' Zinzendorf had no thought of destroying creeds as boundary marks defining the different households of God. Joining with the Moravian brethren, with the Reformed, and with the Lutherans, in sacramental fellowship, he would yet not offer this symbol of fraternity to that great corporation which failed to make a right distinction between believers and unbelievers." When at the age of twenty-one, he purchased Bethelsdorf, and there welcomed the exiled and oppressed Moravian brethren, cast his lot in with them, became their bishop, and moulded the life of the fraternity according to the ancient principles of the *Unitas Fratrum*.

It was a remarkable scene in which Zinzendorf was welcomed to the home of Antes. In training they were just the opposite. The life of Zinzendorf had been in universities, in traveling, in the royal courts, while Antes, who had been partially educated in the schools of Germany, had yet passed the greater part of his life in the American forests. Both were of the same age, Antes being the more robust man of the two. Both were the descendents of nobility, and in their manner gave evidence of the high social habits they had inherited. But these things alone were of little account, their great point of similarity was in the spirit they possessed. Both cherished the same ideal, it seemed to have been born in them, childhood and maturity only adding to its power. Though all the world was against them, they would not hide their desire, but with every nerve sought to give it success. And yet there was this difference, Zinzendorf was more of an ecclesiastic, and was willing to use the paraphernalia of ecclesiasticism, while Antes was ready to discard all that, and with only what the New Testament taught believers to observe, to unite men who were moved by the Spirit of the Lord. In this Antes was superior to Zinzendorf, and at the same time a truer exponent of the ancient principles of the *Unitas Fratrum*, freed from its high church features.

The Count assented to the unity movement rather than positively desiring it, being no doubt, aware of the tremendous obstacles in the way, but after consultations with Antes, Weigner, and others of like mind, who were filled with a strong hope that right might prevail, it was resolved to call a conference, irrespective of denominations, which was done in the following letter.

"Call for a meeting of christians to be held on New Year's Day, 1742, in Germantown. In the name of Jesus! Amen.

"MY DEAR FRIEND AND BROTHER:

Since a fearful injury is done in the Church of Christ among those souls who are called to the Lamb, and this mostly through mistrust and suspicion, and that often without foundation, which one entertains toward another, by which every attempt to do good is frustrated—and since, contrary to this, we are commanded to love one another—the question has been discussed in the minds of some persons for two or more years, whether it would not be possible to bring about a General Assembly, not for the purpose of disputing with one another, but to confer in love on the important articles of faith, in order to see how near all could come together in fundamental points, and in other matters that do not overthrow the ground of salvation, to bear with one another in charity, that thus all judging and condemning among the above mentioned souls might be abated and prevented; since by such uncharitableness we expose ourselves before the world, and give it occasion to say: 'Those who preach peace and conversion themselves stand against one another.' These facts have induced many brethren and God-fearing souls to take this important matter into earnest consideration, and to view it in the presence of the Lord; and they have concluded to assemble on the coming New Year's Day in Germantown. Accordingly, you are heartily entreated, with several others of your brethren who rest on good ground, and can give a reason for their faith, to assemble with us if the Lord permits you so to do. Nearly all others have been informed of this by the same kind of letter as is here sent to you. It is believed that it will be a large Assembly; but let not this keep you back; everything will be done without rumor. The Lord Jesus grant His blessing to it.

From your poor and humble but sincere friend and brother,

HENRY ANTES.

Frederick Township, in Philadelphia Co., Dec. 15, 1741.

It had been decided that Henry Antes should lead the movement, supported by the influence of the others, a position for which they considered him thoroughly qualified, and their confidence was not misplaced. There were seven conferences held. As to the dates, if we adopt the new style, we will place them just eleven days later than the dates on the original documents. The first conference was held at the house of Theobald Entens in Germantown, on the first day of January, 1742. At this meeting Henry Antes presided. Count Zinzendorf was present and had the opportunity for declaring his views, and winning the hearts of the brethren. This meeting continued until late in the evening of the following day, during which questions of doctrine, and the proper basis for christian union were discussed.

The second conference was held at George Hübner's house in Falkner Swamp on January 14th and 15th. At this conference Zinzendorf was also present, and also several who at a later day became prominent in the Moravian interests. Immediately upon the close of this conference Zinzendorf returned to Philadelphia. The third conference met at the house of John de Turck in Oley on the 10th, 11th and 12th of February. This must have been an exceptionally precious meeting, for not only was Zinzendorf present, but he set apart to the work of the ministry, the noble Eschenbach and three of his companions. The fourth conference was at Mr. Ashmead's in Germantown on March 10th, 11th and 12th. At this meeting the wrongs done the Indians at Nazareth was brought forward, and Henry Antes was commissioned to make a thorough examination of the case, and to see that justice was done the Indians. This was indeed a delicate task, owing to the peculiar claims the Indians put forth for lands and privileges which they did not hesitate to sell, and then sell again. The peaceful relations afterward sustained between the Indians and Henry Antes is a proof of how well he executed this delicate diplomatic commission. Zinzendorf was also present at this conference. The fifth conference met at Germantown in April. As this conference was closing, Henry Antes' father married for his second wife Elizabeth Nayman in the First Presbyterian Church in Philadelphia. The sixth conference met in Germantown in May, and the seventh in Philadelphia on June 2nd, 3d and 4th.

The movement met with decided opposition from the start. Denominationalism was fiercely arrayed against it, not only the larger bodies, but the smaller sects also. As this opposition grew many of those who at first desired the success of the movement dropped out of it until it gradually became the property of the Moravians. The opposition stooped to the most unchristian methods. The character of Zinzendorf was assailed and his peculiarities placed in a light to do him harm. Rev. Mr. Boehm put on the war paint and published a pamphlet denouncing Zinzendorf and reproaching Antes, but, while many were frightened from continuing the work, Antes confident in the right of it, as a servant of Jesus Christ could neither be coaxed or frightened out of it. He had adopted it as his life work, and call him what they might, he would persevere, and although not a Moravian at this time, he endorsed Zinzendorf, looked after his interests, and at the seventh meeting of the conference issued an address over his own signature to the people of the Province.

It was entitled "An address of the laborers in the Church of Jesus Christ in Pennsylvania, to the entire country," and it began with the words "Geliebtes Pennsylvania." It is as follows:

"DEAR PENNSYLVANIA:

We, who know you and your circumstances, complained heartily to our brother Von Thurnstein, when he came over the ocean, with such a hungry and thirsty heart for you.

We have seen and felt how rich you are; how satisfied in this matter all are who have an understanding of it; and in what darkness the rest lie. It appeared to us at first, before we understood the deep purpose of wisdom by experience, that his Savior, who is always so true to him, had only permitted the calling together of workers of all religions on one day—which Ludwig more permitted than desired—against all thoughts of men and against all customs of this country, to show him when he had scarcely arrived, as it were, Pennsylvania in a concentrated body together, revealing the bitterness of the rest at once, so that he could from these leaders conclude as to the others, and out of these most properly select the best of the ordinary class. But we were comfortable on the one side, when we heard from him, that, as far as he was concerned, he was only an observer, and should not do anything here but preach the gospel and investigate. It was also to us that he said after his first glance at the religious persuasions: Here a prophet of the Lord would make a frail figure, for here one having a knowledge of the young children's catechism is considered sufficient for the wisdom of these spirits and a match for an honest Lutheran minister. He (Thurnstein) declared quite in the beginning in view of the severe charges against him, and the proscriptions by the congregation who had from him no one to take no care of (*i. e.*, to whom he was under no obligations—they had done him no favors), he saw no person that could be deemed fit, for since in all the wickedness of man the natural want of understanding is the chief cause that men behave so incomprehensibly and frightfully as they do, there could be almost nobody worthy to be admitted into the little congregation (Bundlein), the exclusion therefrom being so unhappy; moreover, up to this time, there had not been a visible congregation in the land, and it was neither reasonable nor evangelical to suppose that the people preferred to look upon the bugbears (pictures of terror they imagined), rather than upon the lovely picture of the church. With this mind he labored; he suffered patiently, he shunned no abuse and words; he would not have answered so fully to Schronfield's writing had he not promised a month previously that he would give arguments if demanded; and to this only had he committed himself; and so soon as he was answered 'here there is nothing to prove except before a court of justice' he allowed the entire multitude of accusations to rest as they were, and contented himself in those days, to prove to us that they were invented word for word. But it is not necessary for us to say more about this brother; there is yet a word for you beloved country people in Pennsylvania. The monthly religious conferences are now at an end. The blessing of God upon our children from Philadelphia and Germantown, who were in the house of our brother, give us much pity that you too have not found worthy an inquiry as to the benevolent act, which was more intended for you than for us, and that the providing for six hundred children was not to be made out so feather easy.* Do then also herein, what pleases your heart, for you are still too rich to need ought, and too proud to ask anything. But we think also of you, hidden people of God in Pennsylvania. To-day at last, a visible congregation of the Lord has been seen and acknowledged in Philadelphia; every member thereof has manifested himself before us. Its home for the present, Bethlehem; the small flocks of evangelical religions, in Philadelphia, Germantown, Oley and Frederick Township who were waiting for the salvation of Israel, which the sectaries call sects, but with whom the most impartial and motherlike spirit is found, have most cordially united with them. Another portion of us belong to such sects as are hirelings to wolves and foxes, and that make robbery of the unfledged chickens of Jesus, if they join invisibly. But we are *one* body, and *one* spirit, *since we are called in one hope;* one *Lord,* one *faith,* one *baptism,* one *God* and *Father of all, who is over us all, and in us all.* We all together constitute the body of Christ in Pennsylvania, which was at our first conference by all religions confessed; at the second again substan-

---

*Perhaps he here means not so easy as the lifting of a feather.

tiated; at the third, sealed; at the fourth, declared; at the fifth and sixth, proved; and at this seventh and last general religions conference, by the visible congregation of Jesus, present, made happy. We shall also continue in all quietness this church council quarterly according as the wisdom of the Lord will supply. Our members will assist in this; to call upon all who are without to acquaint all with the Spirit. HITHERWARD! WHO BELONG TO THE LORD! These are the words of the congregation of the Lord to all their unknown and known fellow members, and all who call upon the Lord our God from their hearts. *You will have pity upon Zion!* By order of the synod.

HENRY ANTES.

Philadelphia, June, 1742.

To show the spirit of the opposition we now present John Philip Boehm's criticisms of Antes, because of his part in the Unity Conferences. "Immediately in the beginning of this account (page B of the authentic account of the proceedings of the Conference held at Germantown, January 2d, 1742) I cannot sufficiently express my astonishment at Henry Antes, who, for several years past for quite exceptional reasons, has separated himself from our Reformed Congregation in Falkner Swamp. With whom I have on several occasions spoken on necessary things, and have, from the tenor of his remarks, lived in strong hope of winning him—which hope I have not yet cast away—although these objectionable* things, which are well known to me, and are going on, and to this date are kept up, but to the good and merciful God I sigh that He will graciously pity him, and all persons confused by the spirit of Dwahling† for the sake of their precious and undying souls. And I will leave to the judgement of every godly and right minded christian what Henry Antes has done, and I exclude none who have done and are doing as he has, and which he continues to do. For, under the clear light of the Gospel was he born, holy baptism did he receive, through which he entered the covenant which He has made for the faithful; this covenant, I doubt not, was explained according to the word of God, for I knew his zealous and faithful instructor well—at his participation in the Holy Communion. At which time, without doubt, he vowed, before his teacher and the elders of the congregation of Christ, and in the presence of the righteous God, that he would persevere to the end of his life and be faithful to our religion (faith) which he had once accepted, and which is grounded upon the true and living God only for salvation through his guiding word. (lee tender worte). This, beloved, which he did before

---

*Literally, " Things going quite against the current of the stream."

†Precisely what Boehm intended by this word we know not. It is probably best translated by the word Mop and may mean as in the Old English provincialism—a grimace; a made up face; or, of the common expression now in use, turning up the nose.

men, and Almighty God, he has broken, and has for several years past, allowed himself to be dragged about by the spirit of Dwahling among all sorts of erring persons, and by their sectarian views. And now at the present time, he allows himself again to be led about like a blind man with a staff, by the more adroit Count von Zinzendorf in his sectarian affairs. To think that Henry Antes, who, as I acknowledge, has a far wider conception (understanding) than many others, would fall into sin before his God, and rejecting His truth, give himself to such a soul destroying teaching (doctrine)! So far as Henry Antes and myself are concerned, he knows full well how our hearts were formerly bound together in cordial love for the divine truth of our Reformed teachings, and that he was one of those who with his tears helped to persuade me to take upon my neck the Yoke.* These things, I am sure, have not passed from his memory. This love, for my part, I have not been able to forget, and although I have been deeply wounded by him, I shall never forget to beseech the Almighty in my prayers, to bring him, together with all the erring ones, by the power of the Holy Ghost, back to the right. But, I would advise him, heartily and openly, if he will receive advice for himself, because it concerns his own undying soul, not to delay too long an honest examination of himself; not to imagine

*Referring to his assuming the ministry without ordination.

such to be unnecessary in his case; it might otherwise, through his own darkening of the heart, be delayed until the end of his life, the nearness of which none of us know. Consider what a sad condition it is for the poor soul, when a person, while it is yet time, is ashamed to acknowledge, from pride of heart that he erred, and afterwards it is too late to retrace the way which had been changed, to the true source of life, in order to be cleansed from the filth with which such person had been besmeared in the stinking puddle-holes."

Chapter XIV.

Indian Tribes on the Border.

THE year 1742 was an eventful year in the life of Henry Antes. His efforts for the establishment of Christian unity had separated him from his pastor and church, and had called down upon him the bitter reproaches of that pastor. It had led him to more and more become the ally of a new sect, but a sect more in harmony with the desires of his own heart. He had found a coterie of companions of exalted religious experience, highly intellectual qualifications, and unwearied zeal for the promulgation of their views. Zinzendorf, Spangenberg, Nitschman, Eschenbach, Weigner, Bohler and Antes, what a company this was! Who can wonder that when together they were inspired with the loftiest desires for the wellbeing of their fellow-men! Antes would not have severed his connection with the Reformed Church, but no other course was open to him, and he was thus led into the fold of these earnest Godly Moravians. All along the course of events we see how they honored him, and also how his influence aided them. In the Unity Conference in Germantown, held March 10th, 11th and 12th of this year

A DELAWARE INDIAN FAMILY.

(1742) Antes was commissioned to make a thorough investigation of the wrongs done the Indians at Nazareth, and to remedy them. From this appointment we conclude that he not only possessed the confidence of the Germans, who had settled at Bethlehem and Nazareth, but also of the Indians whose village occupied that same spot. Moreover it shows that he was familiar with the previous transactions, as indeed we have learned, from his guiding Whitefield to that locality in his purchase. It was essential that the Moravians should be on the most peaceful terms with the Indians, and it shows their great appreciation of the wisdom and the tact of Antes, to give him complete charge of so delicate a mission. From Gordon's history of Pennsylvania we learn how this same trouble was managed by the authorities of the Province. This was well enough for those who by force of arms could compel obedience, but with the Moravians, the Spirit of Christ prevailed, and the Indians were to be treated as brethren.

Gordon says: "During the administration of Governor Thomas (1742) a convention of deputies from the Six Nations, and Delaware Indians, was held at Philadelphia, for the purpose of terminating some dispute which had arisen between the latter tribe and the proprietaries, relative to a cession of lands. A tract, lying in the Forks of the Delaware and Lehigh rivers, extending back into the woods as far as a man can go in a day and a half, denominated the walking purchase, had been sold to William Penn by the Delawares in 1736, and confirmed by the same tribe by their deed, dated 25th of August, 1737. The lines of this purchase having been traced by very expert walkers, and, including more land than the Indians expected, increased the dissatisfaction which had prevailed among them in relation to the grant of 1736. The Indians complained that the walkers, who outstripped them, ran, and did not pursue the course of the river, as they anticipated. The chief, Nutimus, and others, who signed the treaty of 1737, refused to yield peacable possessions of these lands, and declared their intention to maintain themselves by force of arms. Under these circumstances, the proprietaries invoked the interposition of the Six Nations, whose authority over the Delawares was well known. Upon this invitation, a deputation of two hundred and thirty from these powerful tribes visited Philadelphia, where they were met by delegates from the Delawares, who had also been invited. Having heard the complaints of the Governor against the latter, for their retention of the purchased lands, and their misconduct, in writing rude and abusive letters to the proprietaries, Canassatago on the part of the Six Nations said to the Governor 'That they saw the Delawares had been an unruly people, and were altogether in the wrong: that they concluded to remove them, and oblige them to go over the river Delaware (Lehigh) and quit all claims to any lands on this side for the future, since they had received pay for them, and it is gone through their guts long ago. They deserved to be taken by the hair of the head and shaken severely till they recovered their senses and became sober; that he had seen with his eyes a deed signed by nine of their ancestors above fifty years ago for this very land (1686) and a release signed not many years since (1737) by some of themselves, and chiefs then living (Nutimus and Sassoonan then present) to the number of fifteen and upwards; but how come you' continued he to the Delawares, 'to take upon you to sell lands at all? We conquered you; we made women of you; you know you are women, and can no more sell land than women; nor is it fit you should have the power of selling lands, since you would abuse it. This land that you claim has gone through your guts; you have been furnished with clothes, meat, and drink, by the goods paid you for it, and now you want it again, like children as you are. But what makes you sell lands in the dark? Did you ever tell us you had sold this land? Did we ever receive any part, even the value of a pipe shank, from you for it? You have told us a blind story, that you sent a messenger to us, to inform us of the sale; but he never came amongst us, nor did we ever hear anything about it. This is acting in the dark, and not like the custom our Six Nations observe in the sale of lands. On such occasions, they give public notice, and invite all the Indians of their united nations, and give them all a share of the presents they receive for their lands. This is the behavior of the wise united nations. But we find you are none of our blood; you act a dishonest part, not only in this, but in other matters; your ears are ever open to slanderous reports about your brethren. For all these reasons, *we charge you to remove instantly; we don't give you liberty to think about it.* You are women. Take the advice of a wise man and remove instantly. You may return to the other side of the Delaware (Lehigh), where you came from; but we do not know whether, considering how you have demeaned yourselves, you will be permitted to live there, or whether you have not swallowed that land down your throats, as well as the land on this side. We, therefore, assign you two places to go to, either to Wyoming or Shamokin. You may go to either of these places, and then we shall have you more under our eye, and shall see how you behave. *Don't deliberate, but remove away*, and take this belt of wampum.' He then forbid them to intermeddle in land affairs, or ever thereafter pretend to sell any land; and commanded them, as he had something to transact with the English, immediately to depart the council. The Delawares dared not disobey this peremptory command. They immediately left the council, and soon after removed from the Forks; some, it is said, went to Wyoming and Shamokin, and some to the Ohio."

On the 27th of May of this year, there arrived in Philadelphia a colony of Moravians who had sailed from London on March 5th. It numbered fifty-six souls, and was the first "Sea Congregation" of the Moravians that went forth. They came on the snow "Catharine," and, as was to be expected on an ocean journey at that time of the year, when winds were high and icebergs floating on the seas, encountered many mishaps and passed through many dangers. It was a noble company, most of them being married couples. Several of them afterward became distinguished missionaries. The day after their arrival those of the passengers who were not British subjects or had not hitherto been in Pennsylvania, signed the customary obligation of fidelity to the King of Great Britain, and to the Proprietary of the Province and obedience to the laws, and then started on their journey toward Bethlehem, by the way of Henry Antes', whose house they reached at the close of the second day after leaving Philadelphia.

Henry S. Dotterer beautifully says; "In imagination we see the emigrants on their toilsome journey, on that hot Summer's day. Some on horseback, some afoot; clad in the heavy garments from beyond sea; bare-headed women and stalwart men burdened with household treasures; now, they take refuge from the sun's hot rays under the shade of a mighty tree of the forest; then, they bathe their hands and faces in the cooling waters of the rippling stream. About the noonday hour they had crossed hills between the Skippack and the Perkiomen. Now they thread their way along the banks of the latter stream as far as the mouth of Swamp Creek. Here they turn to the left and take a westerly course, keeping close to the creek, for upon it is Antes' mill, their resting place for the night. Towards evening of the second day when the shadows had lengthened, and the cool western breeze fanned their brows, as the sun was sinking behind the encompassing hills, the hour most grateful to the weary travellers, the haven was reached, the noisy mill was before them, the broad meadows of the plantation about them, and the doors of the hospitable home stood wide open. And as darkness closed upon the scene, and the myriad voices of the night made melody, what heartfelt prayers ascended on high, and what blissful rest was there."

How the soul of Antes must have been filled with delight as he welcomed these brethren in the Lord to his home, and songs and rejoicings, prayers and thanksgivings must have welled up sweeter and more full of soul than ever before. It was a glorious hour for Antes and his home.

This was a busy year for Zinzendorf as he zealously upon every opportunity preached the gospel, attended conferences, traveled amongst the Indians, and visited the principal villages of the new country. Antes, too, had his hands, as well as his heart full of work. For such a colony houses were needed; for the carrying out the designs of Zinzendorf skillful workmen were required; Bethlehem was to be established, and towns beyond were to be provided with mills to grind their grain. With his own hands—for he was a skillful mechanic—as well as with his money and advice, Antes assisted in building the grist mill and " Gemein Haus," in Bethlehem, both of these being of logs; he also built a grist mill at Friedensthal (Valley of Peace), and a grist mill and saw mill at Gnaden hutten (Grace dwellings), Another piece of business committed to him was to receive the money from the sale of the vessel which brought the Moravians to Philadelphia after certain expenses were paid, and to expend it for cattle to stock and manure the Nazareth tract. As a business manager they considered him qualified to transact all kinds of affairs, even that which required the most unusual and important exercise of judgment.

During this year an act was passed for the benefit of a certain class of citizens, which greatly helped the better class of German settlers in their rights. It was the outcome of the desire at this time of all parties in authority to secure the good will of the Germans. Prior to the act of 13 Geo. II., the law for the naturalization of persons settling in American colonies, required special bills for the naturalization of all aliens. This act provided that all persons residing seven years in the colonies, taking an oath, or, if Quakers, an affirmation of allegiance and abjuration, and professing the Christian religion as prescribed by the act of the first of William and Mary should be considered as natural born subjects. The Dunkards, Moravians, and Menists, now numerous in the Province, were excluded from the benefit of this act, by their scruples in regard to oaths. To remedy this the act was passed covering as follows, "An act for naturalizing such protestants as are settled, or shall settle within the Province, who, not being of the people called Quakers, do conscientiously refuse the taking of an oath."

While this was being granted, Antes labored at Bethlehem. But in the midst of such labors the spiritual work was not neglected. In the closing Unity Conference it had been decided to hold quarterly conferences, and now, towards the end of September, the first of these was held at his house. It was attended by Rev. Peter Bohler, who had come with the colony in July. It was probably at this conference that Antes announced the contemplated departure of Zinzendorf for Europe in a short time, and his desire to make a preaching tour to the principal centres of population before that time. In this tour Zinzendorf preached at Falkner Swamp (doubtless at the house of Antes), on the seventh of December, from the text, Psalms 130: 3—"If thou, Lord, should'st mark iniquities, O, Lord, who shall stand?" One month and two days from this time, on January 9th, 1743, Zinzendorf sailed from New York to England. But his going was of the deepest interest to Antes, who sent with him his loved daughter in order that she might have the advantages of a better and more christian education than could be obtained in the Province.

What a trial this must have been. Anna Margaretta, Antes' second daughter, was only fourteen years of age. She was a child of great natural talent and received much attention from the Moravian leaders, as was seen in the way in which she held the position given her in her maturer years. She was now sent to the Moravian school in London to complete her education. There in after years she became the wife of the Moravian preacher, Rev. Benjamin Latrobe, and one year after her marriage, 1767, became the mother of one, who was the architect of that part of the Capitol of the United States, at Washington, built previous to 1817, that is, he designed the central building, the wings being afterward added, they being the work of Thomas U. Walters.

How interesting that when the government of

the United States desired to build its Capitol, it should secure as architect the grandson of the mechanic who was the builder of the plain log mills and houses of Bethlehem. The year following the departure of his daughter and the Count, Antes spent in ministering to the Moravians dwelling in Oley, a few miles from his home. This year was made memorable by a production that must have filled the heart of the preacher with deepest joy. That was the printing of a German Bible.

In Germantown the Germans had established a printing house, and as early as 1738 published almanacs, school books, and various kinds of religious works. In 1739 Christopher Sower commenced his *Hoch Deutsch Pennsylvanische Geschichtes schreiber*, the first newspaper printed in the Province of Pennsylvania. The almanac printed in 1738 in both size and matter was far superior to those that had preceded it in English. But now a great advance was made by Mr. Sower in printing a magnificent edition of 1200 copies of the Bible, each containing 1,284 quarto pages. This preceded the publication of an English Bible in Philadelphia by thirty-seven years. This Bible was thoroughly the work of Germans. They made the ink, cast the type, made the paper, did the binding, and paid all the expense of the work, and then stood by the brave printer by purchasing the copies, which he printed, so that within twenty years a second and larger edition was necessary. Antes could now go on in his work with the power of the printing press within the reach of his people, and that press dedicated to the service of God.

Chapter XV.

Moravian Schools and Education.

THE year 1743 was spent by Antes in earnest work among a peaceful people, while in Philadelphia the Assembly was carrying its point in opposition to the Governor by starving him out, and they only consented to pay his salary when he submitted, at least partially, to their will. Antes seems to have spent a quiet year also in 1744, during which he presided at a synod held in what is now North Heidleberg township, in November, and on the 4th of that same month attended the dedication of a Moravian Church built the preceding Summer. But this year was one of trouble to the Province, for a masked and indirect war had been for some time carried on between France and Great Britain, and hostilities were openly declared by the former on the 20th, and by the latter on the 31st of March. At this time Philadelphia was supposed to have at least 1,500 houses and 13,000 inhabitants. "On June 11th war against France was formally proclaimed at the court house by the Governor, Mayor, and Corporation. The Governor, by proclamation, ordered every one capable of bearing arms to provide himself with firelock, bayonet, cartouche box, and powder and ball enough to defend the Province and annoy the enemy. When the Assembly met all talk took a martial guise, and the Governor put many puzzling questions to a legislative body in which the Quakers were a majority. He recounted the insolence of a French privateer, the captain of which sent a message from the Capes to the effect that he knew Philadelphia too well to be afraid they would send to pursue him, and announcing that he meant to stay there two weeks longer. The Assembly, however, said nothing, and the Corporation Council petitioned the king to consider and relieve the defenceless condition of the city, exposed to attack from its position on the sea-board, and undefended in consequence of the religious scruples of the inhabitants. The people, however, were not so peaceful as the Assembly. The streets were picturesque with war scenes. Troops were recruiting for several expeditions, and the privateersmen beat up the town for volunteers."

"The exertions of Franklin at this time contributed greatly to the security of the Province, and to the preservation of harmony between the executive and Assembly. He published a pamphlet entitled 'Plain Truth,' exhibiting in strong lights the helpless state of the Province, and the necessity of union and discipline. Calling a meeting of the citizens, he laid before them a plan for a military association; 1,200 signatures were immediately procured, and the volunteers soon amounted to 10,000, armed at their own expense, and officered by their own choice. This tract was published also in German, and the first company fully organized was a company of Germans. Franklin was chosen colonel of the Philadelphia regiment, but, declining the service, Alderman Lawrence was elected on his recommendation. By Franklin's means, also, a battery was erected below the city, from funds raised by lottery, in which Logan and many other Quakers were adventurers. Logan, who was not scrupulous in relation to defensive war, directed whatever prizes he might draw should be applied to the service of the battery. These military preparations were necessary to intimidate a foreign enemy, and to curb the hostile disposition of the Indians, which had been awakened by several unpleasant recontres with the whites."

It was thoroughly essential at this time to keep on the best of terms with the Indians, and no measures were left untried to take from them all cause of complaint. At this time (1745) the French were tampering with the Six Nations, whom they would have liked to see putting on the war paint and murdering the settlers in the frontier, but the Six Nations had no desire to do so, and remained neutral, but the suspicion that they might be aroused, created terror in the Province.

In the midst of these alarms Henry Antes proceeded with his work, holding the confidence of all who knew him. January 8th of this year his sixth son was born, whom he named Joseph. During the Spring of this year he attended a large church council at Muddy Creek. On the second week in March, the Moravian Synod held their session in his house. At this session the question of education assumed a prominent place, and as a result of their deliberations, Antes made the remarkable sacrifice of offering his house, plantation, mill, and buildings for the use of the Brethren as a boarding school for boys. The offer was accepted at once, and on the 3d of the following June the school was opened. Christopher and Christina Francke, of Bethlehem, were placed in charge of the undertaking; a tutor, and manager of the farm and mill—which were to be worked for the benefit of the institution — were appointed. Twenty-three pupils were brought from Bethlehem and Nazareth, and eleven others entered in 1745. Among the pupils the first year were white boys from New York, Philadelphia, and various places in Pennsylvania, a Mohegan Indian and a negro from St. Thomas. In the years following a number more of Indians and negroes were taught in this school. Having thus given up his property to the use of the Brethren, Henry Antes removed his household—except his two sons left in the school—to Bethlehem, in order that he might devote his entire time to the service of the growing community.

On December 15th, 1745, he was appointed a justice of the peace for Bucks county. This appointment was renewed in 1749, and in 1752, having returned to Philadelphia county (now Montgomery county), he was again appointed to this office; so that from the time of his appointment until his death, he served on the board of justices of the Province. During the colonial period the justices were appointed by the governors, or the lieutenant-governor, and they were therefore supposed to be known as men well qualified for such honorable positions, and yet they were not always supposed to be versed in legal lore. The profession of the law was not held in as high honor as it is to-day. But the justice was held in much higher honor. A justice was a very important personage, and to him was committed a supervision of public affairs that embraced what is now given to a number of officials. "They were to keep the peace within their jurisdiction, and to keep and cause to be kept all ordinances and statutes, for the good of the peace, and for the preservation of the same, and for the quiet rule and government of our people. To chastise and punish all persons that offend against the ordinances and statutes, such as all manner of felonies, poisonings, inchantments, sorceries, and magick, trespasses, forestallings, regratings, ingrossings, and sorceries whatsoever. * * And also of all those who, in companies against our peace, in disturbance of our people, with armed force have gone or rode, or hereafter shall presume to go or ride; and also of all those who have lain in wait, or hereafter shall presume to lay in wait, to maim or cut or kill our people, and also of all victuallers and all other persons who in the abuse of weights and measures, or in selling victuals against the form of the ordinance, &c., &c."

The minute nature of their supervision can be understood from this law; "Whereas, it has been the practice of tavern keepers, ale house keepers, inn-holders to exact excessive rates for their beer, cyder, and other liquors, and also provender for horses without regard to the plenty or cheapness thereof; be it therefore enacted that the justices of the peace of the respective counties of this Province, shall have full power four times in the year, to wit: at the general sessions of the peace, held for the said counties respectively, to set such reasonable prices in all liquors retailed in public houses, and provender for horses in public stables from time to time as they shall see fit; which prices shall be proclaimed by the cryer at the conclusion of their said respective sessions and fixed upon the court house doors for public view."

Court was held by the body of the justices of the county, the senior in office being the presiding judge. They were supposed to be competent for their duties, hence an appeal would be a rare event. In all the Province who was better qualified for this position than Henry Antes, who by his associations with others knew every Indian trail, and had watched the settlements as they grew and changed under the labor of the neighbors to whom he had proclaimed the eternal righteousness of Christ?

In these early times it was no sinecure, misunderstandings in regard to titles and boundaries were sure to rise, and it required a level judgment to discern the right of the case. But, moreover, if we accept the general view of the nature of the inflocking population, there must have been need for strict watchfulness that the worthless, idle, and dishonest among them should be repressed, and by the fear of the law be kept from violating its precepts.

At this time the justices were often engaged in trying cases produced by disputes and conflicts along the rivers. This was particularly the case on the Schuylkill River. Those who lived along the shore built racks, wears or dams which seriously interfered with navigation, for the people who lived in the regions above the river, and in the outer settlements loaded their canoes with wheat and thus brought it to the market in Philadelphia. Some of these canoes were of immense size, and as a canoe was made of a single log, it is an evidence of the size of the timber then growing along the rivers. One canoe injured by a fish rack was ladened with one hundred and forty bushels of wheat. William Penn tells of a canoe that was made from a poplar tree which carried four tons of bricks. At length the contests between the settlers along the shore who built the fish racks, etc., and the farmers who brought their produce down in canoes became so bitter that the canoes came down in fleets—what an imposing sight that must have been! and by the number of men with them defied the shore men. In this way they destroyed many racks, but the shore men also congregated in crowds, and whenever a canoe was caught in a rack, stoned the occupants and endeavored to destroy the canoe. For ten years this continued until by a proclamation of James Logan, the sheriffs of the counties along the Schuylkill were commanded to suppress the racks, etc., and free the river for navigation. While Antes was a justice in Philadelphia county he more or less came in contact with these river troubles, for it required many years to secure the freedom of the river.

This same year 1746 Frederick Antes, Henry's father, died and was buried on his farm in New Hanover township. It was only the year before that William Dewees, the father of Henry's wife, died and was buried in Germantown. Both lived to see the beginning of the greatness of their beloved son.

Chapter XVI.

Henry Antes' Labors for the Moravians.

THE year 1746 was also full of important incidents to Henry Antes. In April he became one of the trustees of the Moravian Church property on Sassafras (Race) street, above Second, in Philadelphia. In July his heart was made glad by once more meeting the eloquent Whitefield, and taking him with his retinue to visit the Moravian settlements. Starting from Bethlehem, they proceeded to Nazareth, where Whitefield had so fondly hoped to establish a school, and now had the pleasure of seeing a flourishing school in the best of hands, then they passed over to Gnadenthal, and returned to Bethlehem. The five years since these two great men had met had been full of changes and stirring events for both, but their zeal had not relaxed, and their love for the Lord knew no waning.

In less than a month after this delightful visit, Antes' house was touched with the cloud of affliction, but his house was not alone. In the Spring and Summer of this year an epidemic disease of great malignity raged through New England, New York, New Jersey, and Pennsylvania; Dr. John Kearsley called it the *angina maligna*, or putrid sore throat, the traits of the disease as described being similar to those of diphtheria. Its epidemic character was supposed to be due to atmospheric causes. The science of medicine at that day was entirely unable to cope with it, and such practice at this day would be considered barbarous and destructive. They sought to destroy the disease by bloodletting and the use of mercurials, but the disease spread so rapidly that many villages were almost depopulated. It was while this scourge was raging that death entered the house of Antes and took their youngest, their babe. This was the second time death had entered his fold.

It was during this year and the year following that the merchant service on the seas was so greatly hindered by privateersmen. While the English preyed on the French and Spanish, the French and Spanish preyed on the English. A privateer from Philadelphia was captured by the enemy and several French privateers entered Delaware Bay. Great excitement was caused by these events, and the entire Province was in a state of constant alarm. The French and English were both endeavoring to win the assistance of the formidable Six Nations against the other, and this too caused a great sensitiveness as to what ever was done affecting the loyalty of the Indians toward the English.

Just at this juncture, some enemy of the Moravians spread the report that they were in league with the French and Indians, and that the Gemein Haus at Bethlehem was used as an arsenal in which they had stored three thousand stand of arms, for the use of the Indians, who should join the French in making inroads into Pennsylvania. Such a report would naturally arouse great feeling, and this with the accompanying suspicion, would be intensified, because of the mystery involved in the customs of the Moravians, and their peculiar family arrangements so far off in the wilderness as the Forks of the Delaware. The consequence was that an investigation was ordered, and the examining council met at Newtown in Bucks county, Pennsylvania. Henry Antes appeared as the deputy and defender of the Moravians. There was a large assembly, and their interest was riveted upon Antes when he arose to speak. A large, noble looking man, fully appreciating the importance of the occasion, a justice of the Province, a Moravian preacher, in the very prime of life, thoroughly acquainted with Indian affairs, with his work and influence stretching from Philadelphia to the Blue Mountains, having the confidence of the officers of the Province and of the Indians, he was one to whom they would naturally listen, and with the more respect because he earned his living entirely aside from his public positions. He was a miller and a farmer, and in full sympathy with the settlers who were making their homes in the wilderness by daily, strenuous toil.

What he said we do not know, but the result was he proved the entire innocence of the Moravians, and fastened the crime of perjury upon the accuser, upon whom a heavy fine was imposed. Then another feature of the deputy's character appeared. He pleaded for the pardon of the perjurer until the fine was remitted, and then turned to the large assembly and bore a prompt testimony concerning Jesus Christ our Savior, and as a preacher of the Gospel urged them to make their peace with God through Jesus. Thus he turned this occasion of false accusation into a great victory for the truth.

The following year, he and his wife united with the Moravian family near Gnadenthal, probably at this time building the mill for them, and establishing them upon a firm foundation. What beautiful names the Moravians gave their towns, how refreshing to their wearied souls must have sounded the name Gnadenthal (valley of grace), and how all of these names must have encouraged the hearts of the Brethren in Europe as they so longingly turned their eyes toward America.

In 1748 they returned to Bethlehem to live, and at once became members of that Economy again. At this time the highway between Philadelphia and the Minisink valley, and thence on to the north-west part of the Province of New York passed through Bethlehem and the wind gap of the Blue Mountains. The west branch of the Delaware—now the

Lehigh—was wide and difficult to cross when the stream was full, and the only way of crossing was by small boats owned by individuals, or fording. In this year on the 18th of February, the Proprietaries granted Henry Antes license to construct a ferry, to be used for seven years for the use of the Brethren. This ferry carried all the people—Indians, settlers, and travelers who passed along that prominent route. It was the one great ferry on the Lehigh, toward which the forest paths necessarily converged.

On the 29th of May, the Snow Irene, built on Staten Island, was launched and registered in Henry Antes' name. This was a vessel equipped with two masts resembling the main and fore-masts of a ship, and a third small mast just abaft the main-mast carrying a try-sail. Henry Antes accordingly went to New York for the purpose of attending this launch, for the ship building interests of the Moravians were of considerable importance. It was difficult at that early time to give proper care to emigrants in coming to the colonies, there were so many land sharks to deceive and take advantage of the ignorance of the emigrants. But the Moravians sought to remedy this by owning and working their own line of vessels, and this vessel was one of the number. So that we see Henry Antes was more than a Provincial man, he was an international worker for justice. We can imagine the interest his visit must have caused in the city of less than 30,000 inhabitants, which was struggling to possess the shipping trade of the continent. For as the business manager of the ardent Moravians he would appear in the city of business as the all important personage.

On the 16th of September of this year, he records, "To-day a little daughter was born to me in Bethlehem, about two o'clock in the morning. I named her Benigna. On this day she was baptized into the family of God; May the slain Lamb receive and retain her at his open wounded side." Benigna was the name of the wife of Count Zinzendorf, and thus we learn she must have made a very favorable impression on the mind of Antes. This was his eleventh and last child. When only twelve years of age she died at Bethlehem and her Savior received her.

On the 27th of October Antes received another mark of the confidence of the Brethren by being appointed *Consenior Civilis* or business manager of the Moravian establishment at Bethlehem, requiring him to take the legal care of all the property, and the outward temporal affairs of the community. How well he was fitted for this office. He was a citizen possessing all the civil rights of any citizen of the Province; the justice of that section, and fully acquainted with all the legal duties required; a man of wealth and thus able to assume the responsibility for the welfare of that committed to his trust; and in thorough sympathy with the Brethren, his heart was also enlisted in their favor. What more could they expect of an officer?

Now he buys property, erects buildings, enters into contracts, devises plans, appears before the government of the Province, in fact does all their business in his own name, and yet it was all their own. Never was there the least insinuation of the wrong use of even a penny, his trust was sacred. As an indication of the manner in which he labored we learn on November 11th of this year, in company with Bishop Spangenberg and John Watteville, he proceeds to Nazareth to examine the building known as the "Stone House," to see if it would afford suitable accommodations for the infants of the church, who at this time were collected together in the Nursery at Bethlehem. It was found to be suitable and on the 7th of January of the following year the infants were removed to the "Stone House." It was as Superintendent of the Single Sisters and Girls at Nazareth and Bethlehem that Ann Catharine, his eldest child, spent several years of her useful life.

It was during this same year that there appeared another evidence of the labor and zeal of the Germans for the religion so dear to their hearts. This, however, was not by the Moravians, but by the Dunkard Brethren at Ephrata. It was the translation and publication of Van Braght's *Blutige Schau-platz oder Martyrer Spiegel* from the Dutch. It was a wonderful undertaking, 1500 pages (folios), and in magnitude exceeded all works previously published in this country. Its subject was "The Persecution of the Christians from the Time of Christ to the Year 1660." In order to produce it fifteen men labored on it, giving all their time to it, for three years. To possess such a work must have stirred the heart of every German who loved the history of his martyr ancestors, and the accomplishment of so great a work made a profound impression upon the mind of Franklin, the philosopher, statesman, and editor, who fully realized the nature of such an undertaking. German persistence and endurance in the line of their conviction, and for their religion was unsurpassed.

Chapter XVII.

Separation from the Moravians. Return to his Home in Frederick. Appointed Justice in Philadelphia County. His Trip to North Carolina.

HAVING thus far traced the course of the life of this prominent man, we have found him to be endowed with such faculties as well fitted him for an adviser and a leader of the people. With a great heart, loving his friends intensely, but his Lord and Savior more, ready to make any amount of personal sacrifice in order to serve his Master and his fellow men, and in the midst of all manner of opportunities for self aggrandizement, keeping himself unspotted from the world. As we see him the loving companion of Spangenberg, of Nitschman, of Zeisberger, men of purest character and indisputable zeal for the Lord, we naturally think that nothing but death could sever such strong and reciprocated ties, and yet, strange as it may seem, there was a severance of the ties that bound them—not the ties of friendship, but the ties of fellowship in the work of the Lord—and the severance was sharp, emphatic, and irreversible. It sorely grieved the hearts of all parties, and yet for *conscience sake*, Antes felt that he could not return to the fold he had done so much to establish. He allowed his children to follow the dictates of their own conscience. Some of them remained with the Moravians, and some went with the Reformed Church.

John Philip Boehm, his former pastor in the Reformed Church, had died a year before, and to no other minister of that church could Antes turn for comfort in this hour of trial. Possibly all looked dark about him. Things were so different from the days of his youth. The aim of his life seemed to be more distant than ever. Failure seemed to mark all that he had done for the unification of his Christian brethren in the German churches. And yet, so strong were his convictions, so lofty was his ideal, so earnest were his hopes, that he swerved not a hair' breadth from the line of his convictions as to the true life. He might die with failure menacing all his plans, but some time or other God would bring it to pass. He would rest in hope that all the children of God will sometime dwell together in harmony, peace and love, and there will be no sects, but the world will see an undivided and resistless church. The account of the separation from the Brethren is very short. "In April, 1750, the Moravians at Bethlehem introduced the wearing of the white robe or surplice by the minister, at the celebration of the Eucharist. Henry Antes disapproved of this, and withdrew from their communion."

Many will say it was a small thing to cause so great a trouble — perhaps to them it might be small — a bullet riddled flag of the Pennsylvania Reserves would be a small affair to a citizen of London, but not to that regiment in the field of battle. The surplice was a great affair because of what it represented. To those ambitious Moravians it meant an additional attraction in their worship, while to Antes it would detract from their spiritual worship of God; to them it meant the elevation of the ministry to a position of more appreciation or reverence, to Antes it made the ministry a sacerdotal class, and no longer merely the Brethren; to them it meant the establishment of a symbol which would add to the significance of the ordinance, to Antes it was a violation of the spirituality and simplicity of the Moravian worship which was to be the foundation for universal christian union, and by adding to the ordinance took away what properly belonged thereto; to them it was an improvement coming with the spirit of culture and success which had blest them, and a return to the custom observed in Europe since 1457, while to Antes it was the destruction of the object of their union adapted to the free life in the Province, and a surrendering to the spirit of the world, which beginning in this small way, would widen until the *Unitas Fratrum* would in no ways be superior to the denominations of christians about them but like them be made useless by over-spreading formalism. No! He could not approve of it. It demanded his most intense opposition, and this could best be manifested by his withdrawal from their community. He announced his intention, no compromise could be made, and the preparations for his departure from Bethlehem were at once begun.

Thus once more for conscience sake he gives up his home, his beloved companions, and his position as *Consensior Civilis*. What changes it also made in the school at his home in Frederick. The school was broken up, the scholars were transferred to other schools, and with his family Antes returned to his farm and his mill to lament the estrangement from the Brethren and do what lay nearest his hand. But so valuable a man could not be allowed to remain idle, and on May 25th, 1752, he was appointed justice of the peace in Philadelphia county, of which county at this time Frederick township was a part. What pleasure it must have given his old friends to receive him amongst them once more. In a new settlement like that a few years would make a great change in the appearance of things, but Antes was not a stranger to these changes.

It was only about twenty-five miles from Bethlehem to his home, and was almost one neighborhood in those days when miles were so little thought of, and as Moravians dwelt all through that section, his position as manager would have kept him in continued communication with them all. And this too would enable them to frequently visit each other, but we do not know that any such visits took place. The feelings were too deeply lacerated, but at length a break occurred, and the story of it with its results is given in the following account by his son, the missionary John Antes, who after the breach continued as before devotedly attached to the Moravian Church.

*" Towards the close of the year 1752, a proposal was made to Brother Spangenberg that in company with some of the Brethren of a business tact, he should select and have surveyed land in North Carolina which the Brethren had bought for the purpose. In the Life of Spangenberg, an account of the journey is given. The company consisted of Bishop Spangenberg, Henry Antes, Timothy Horsefield, Joseph Miller, Herman Loesch and John Merk."

The account is as follows: †" On the 25th of August, 1752, they entered upon the long, tedious and dangerous journey. They made their way through Virginia to the town of Edenton in North Carolina, and there consulted with the agent of Lord Granville (the owner of the land). They arrived here in safety and good health on the 10th

*Translated from the German by H. S. Dotterer.

†Translated by H. S. Dotterer.

of September, having had thus far good roads
and pleasant weather for traveling; although now
and then there had been scarcity of food for their
horses, and all their necessaries had generally cost
them high prices. From Edenton, taking with
them the surveyor of the Province, they journeyed
toward the Catawba river. On the way they visited
the Indian town of the Tuscaroras, by whom they
were received in a friendly manner. They pro
ceeded farther, and on the 21st came to a house in
which they were greeted with a loving welcome.
Here all the Brethren except one, were prostrated
by fever, which compelled them to halt an entire
week. As soon as they were somewhat improved
they continued their journey. Spangenberg was
yet extremely weak, and they had scarcely pro
ceeded a mile when he fainted, so that the Brethren
had to lead him to the next house, where with one
brother he remained over night, the other members
of the company, on account of scarcity of room,
being obliged to return to their former stopping
place. The next morning he wrote them they
should come; the Savior would certainly grant him
the requisite strength. The beloved man was,
however, so weak that he had to dismount from his
horse a number of times to recline upon the ground
when he had rested somewhat, they assisted him
again upon his horse. In this way, with much diffi
culty they reached the house of an English acquain-

tance where they left a Brother (Horsefield) whom the fever would not leave, with another (Miller) as attendant. Spangenberg with the three remaining Brethren, continued the journey, and took, besides the surveyor, two hunters, partly to carry the surveyor's chains and partly to shoot game for them in the forests. They now gradually improved in health from day to day, as he had foreseen, and they arrived during the last half of October in good condition in a somewhat populated neighborhood on the Catawba River, about two hundred and forty miles from Edenton. Up to this time they had at least met a house at the close of every day, in which to quarter for the night, but now their course lay through a trackless wilderness, in which they were to select and survey the land. They provided themselves here with a fourteen days' supply of provisions, for that they should have to spend fourteen weeks in this forest region, not one supposed. On the second of November they proceeded farther, with the words of the 107th Psalm in their minds and on their lips. 'They wandered in the wilderness in a solitary way; they found no city to dwell in. Hungry and thirsty their soul fainted in them. Then they cried unto the Lord in their trouble, and he relieved them out of their distresses. And he led them forth by the right way, that they might go to a city of habitation.' They soon found a good tract of land, but consumed five days in surveying one thousand acres; for the streams which ran through it were so deep that they could neither descend nor ascend the high steep banks, and in order to get across they had first to seek a path made by buffaloes; and although they were frequently obliged to use such paths, yet great caution was necessary because they occasionally led into deep marshes. The farther they proceeded with the survey, the more perilous became the work; the Winter came upon them, and they were obliged to spend the nights in their tents. In going according to the compass they soon came to thick, almost impenetrable forests; now they had fearful precipitous mountains to ascend and descend, and this continued for about forty miles. Now the men often relieved the horses of the weight of the effects and implements, and themselves carried these burdens up the mountains beside dangerous precipices.

"On the 29th of November,' says their journal, 'we encamped in a neighborhood to which perhaps from the creation of the world no human being had come; upon fearful mountains, where neither track nor path was to be seen. Yet are we, praised be God, all well, hearty, contented and thankful for our Heavenly Father's care and keeping, and for the company of the holy angels who thus far have attended us and our people, of which we have ample evidence.'

"At last they could no longer use the compass, inasmuch as they came to a stream whose course they must follow, which however led them so far into the mountains that even the hunters, who were to be their guides, became discouraged, and gave up the hope of getting out of them again. Their supply of bread, notwithstanding the small allowance dealt out, towards the last, was now exhausted, and they subsisted entirely upon game, which the hunters from time to time secured in the forest. It even came at one time to this that they could find no food for their horses, and that they themselves had been the third day without anything to eat. A fresh stream which they followed led them at last into a grassy spot, and the hunters killed two stags. Here was joy! They now recovered their spirits, and they came toward the end of December, to the Yadkin. Upon the opposite side of the river they saw white people, who called to them and offered them shelter. In another day they succeeded in crossing the water, although not without risk, remained several days with these people, and satisfied their hunger. One of the inhabitants brought them to the vicinity where now Wachovia lies. Here they found what they sought. They were directed to the tract they had previously surveyed, and they now took up the 100,000 acres. On the 13th of January, 1753, they completed the surveys. Although this occurred in the middle of

Winter, in a snow of considerable depth, and they encamped all the time in the woods, yet they were well and in good spirits (under the care and guardianship of their dear Lord). On the 12th of February they returned to Bethlehem."

This was Henry Antes' last act in the service of the Moravians, for whom he had done so much, and whom he loved so devotedly, and it was a service which hastened the close of his useful life. Although in his prime he was a strong and hearty man, the severity of his labors, the privations he had endured in the wilderness, and accidents suffered in the performance of his work, with the weight of the responsibility of the trust he upheld, broke down his strong constitution, and shortened his valuable life.

Chapter XVIII.

The London School Movement.

THE year 1754 saw the beginning of a new work promising the greatest advantages to the future influence and well-being of the German settlers. Thus far they had been constantly looked upon with suspicion by the English in Philadelphia. Although at all times we find that Antes, their defender, was held by the English authorities in the greatest confidence and respect, as he stood as a shield for his weaker Brethren. But Antes could enter into speech and correspondence with the English, while the most of his fellow Germans could not, and in this inability appeared their disadvantage. The tenacity with which they held to their mother tongue, did indeed seem like the establishing of a foreign community in the new State, and was, and would be contrary to the expectations of the Founder, and in order to have that political unity, which could alone make the Province powerful, the people must be one in speech and customs, as well as in the desire for personal liberty. The tenacity of the Germans for their own ways and speech seemed to blind them to this fact, but already such observing broad-minded men as Antes plainly discerned the case. They saw that the Germans for self protection and future usefulness must learn English. In Philadelphia two days of the week were market days, and once a year the Provincial Fair, in imitation of the old English Fairs was held. This Fair day was generally used as a holiday and was given to hireing help, making bargains, and having a good time generally. Because of their agricultural occupations the Germans were largely drawn to these, and in bargaining English was a necessity.

Just at this time another influence was brought to bear on this subject. A company was formed in London for the purpose of establishing English schools among the Germans, and the dissemination of the gospel to them in that tongue. The importance of that movement can be appreciated when we remember that while the older ones would never learn the strange language, their children, being surrounded with English speech and customs, would necessarily learn it, or if not, they would not be able to sustain themselves in society or in business, and as the new language replaced the old, unless churches were formed for them, and the gospel preached to them in English, they would drift into other communions, or out of a religious life because of their dislike of the more primitive language. This same battle is fought over and over again in every land where this transition occurs, and in nearly all cases the breach becomes the wider because of the refusal of the parents to accept the inevitable for the sake of their children.

Henry Melchior Muhlenberg was the instrument in the hands of the London Society to advance this work. Let us look at his career for a moment. He was one of the followers of the Pietistic movement in Germany, although not a Pietist in the strict sense of placing his evangelism above church relations. He was a great churchman and was sent to America in 1742 to gather the Lutherans into folds and shepherd them. His energy knew no cessation; he, like a skillful general, grasped the whole country, and sought to bring it under his control. When he came to the neighborhood where Antes lived, in New Hanover, he found one hundred communicants of his denomination worshipping in a log meeting house. He was met by considerable opposition from self-constituted preachers, but by his tact and eloquence overcame all their influences, and at once pushed the work forward with ever-increasing strength. With Muhlenberg and Antes there were many strong ties, as aside from their denominationalism they were of one mind and one heart in the elevation of the German people.

The historian says of Muhlenberg, and this will at once show his union with Antes: "He traveled far and wide, responding to the call of duty among the churches from New York to Georgia. He preached in churches, in private houses, in the open air, and carried the gospel from house to house in pastoral visitation. He adapted himself to the wants and tastes of the people. He was able to preach in either the German, Dutch or English language, sometimes using all three the same day. Had his wise policy been pursued by his immediate successors, much of the work performed by him and his co-laborers would not have been lost to the church of which they were members; but those coming after them, confining their ministrations to the German language were not able to hold those who were growing up under the influence and training of the English language and customs. Every means by which piety could be cultivated was practiced by pastor Muhlenberg. Immediately on his arrival in this country he organized prayer meetings for the edification of the church; these he could seldom attend. They were held often—three times each week—some pious laymen presiding. Prayers were offered, the Bible and books of religious value were read. So marked were these meetings that the wicked sometimes made it an object to disturb them by casting stones against the door, and by reviling the worshippers as pietists and hypocrits. He was a promotor of revivals of religion. The interest which the people took in their preaching during such efforts was manifested by the 'audible weeping of the congregation and the advice sought in private concerning the salvation of their souls.' Muhlenberg had no stated forms by which worship should be invariably conducted. When he used a liturgical service it was short and simple, but he believed that a minister should be bound to no system. In all his services his object was to lead men to Christ, so he adopted any method that would bring about the desired end. His preaching was plain and simple. He used both the formal discourse and the more practical method of question and answer. Sometimes, immediately after the sermon, the congregation was questioned on the leading points presented in it; they were requested to find the proof texts, which led them to bring their Bibles to church. The afternoon hour was frequently employed in question and answer, the subject being either the morning sermon or some other portion of the Bible or catechism. He expressed his notion of preaching as follows: 'In our discourses we ought to make no ostentatious display of learning, but study simplicity. We should neither strike into the air, nor employ low and vulgar expressions, nor introduce too much matter into a sermon, but discuss the subject fully, and apply it to the heart. Our sermons should not be dry, but practical. Religion should be presented not as a burden, but as a pleasure. Let us sow with tears, let us aim at the edification of each individual soul, and give heed to ourselves and to our doctrines.' Muhlenberg, with his coworkers, was never satisfied until he had brought those under his instruction into full christian experience. He everywhere insisted on rigid discipline. His strict views concerning the sanctity of the Sabbath in many places brought him into trouble with those who looked upon it as a day for general recreation and amusement. Of the general results of their labors he and his associates in the ministry declare that with the middle-aged, who have grown up without instruction, they were unsuccessful, but from the young they derived great encouragement."

To show still further how this great man and Antes thought alike, we quote Muhlenberg's own language after the meeting of one of the conferences which he had established. "After the close of public worship all the ministers convened at my house, and held a biblical colloquy on the essential characteristics of genuine repentance, faith, and godliness, in which they endeavored to benefit each other, according to the grace given them, by communicating the results of their own experience and self-examination, so that it was a cheering and delightful season. The residue of the evening was spent in singing spiritual hymns and psalms, and in conversation about the spiritual condition of our churches, and so short did the time appear, that it was three o'clock in the morning before we retired to rest. Oh, how delightful it is when ministers, standing aloof from all political and party contests, seek to please their Lord and Master Jesus Christ, and have at heart the welfare of their churches and the souls entrusted to their care, and are willing rather to suffer reproach with the people of God than choose the treasures of Egypt." Such was the man who now undertook the work of leading the Germans to study the English language.

He had antagonized Antes on the unity movement, and although belonging to a different communion, recognized the great influence Antes possessed, and yet both of these men were so reasonable that they laid aside all natural predjudice and suspicion, and when Muhlenberg called on Antes to aid him in this work, Antes responded by throwing his whole heart into it. In a note to Rev. William Smith, Muhlenberg gives an account of the meeting held in New Hanover respecting the proposed schools, in which he says: "I delivered * * all your other papers into the hands of Henry Antes, Esq., who, being a man of great reputation and influence, was attentively heard while he explained the same to the people. After conferring a litte together they (Reformed) all melted at once into tears of joy, uttered many thankful expressions, and agreed in christian harmony in the choice of our Lutheran school-house, also their own school-house, which is only about sixty poles distant." This shows that Antes had returned to the fellowship of his beloved Reformed communion, and had not lost a particle of his influence with them, and was now able to lead his church to fraternize with the Lutherans, a movement requiring the most delicate management. In his soul there was no room for harboring resentments or standing on trifles, and in all things he was ready to go with them just as far as his conscience was not offended. In this incident we also see how in that early day, the followers of the Pietists in Germany were brought into associations with each other in America, and carried out the principles of their Master, the Lord Jesus Christ, within their denominational lives, in the most thorough and consistent manner. To them Christ was superior to all personal desires.

But notwithstanding the earnest efforts of these men, backed by the London Society, the movement was, like the unity movement, severely antagonized by not only the more ignorant of the Germans, but also by those who sought to curry favor with them, and maintain a political influence over them. Then, as to-day, the power of the press was second to no other, and the German newspaper published by Sauer, in Germantown, while esteeming Antes most highly, threw its influence against the movement, and being in harmony with the predjudices of the people, so influenced them that the effort proved a failure. Then, as to-day, the newspaper was merely the exponent of the prevalent sentiment of the times, while Antes and the others were filled with the spirit of a later and a more advanced day.

In Philadelphia, the antagonism between the Governor and the Quakers in the Assembly seemed to be perpetual, and strife marked almost every step of progress that was taken. As the Germans mostly sided with the Quakers, there were frequent charges of disloyalty aimed at them, and because they were true and loyal, this hurt their feelings, and led them to justify themselves. "On the 20th of November 1754, the principal German protestants of the Province addressed a letter to the Hon. Robert Hunter Morris, Esq., Lieutenant Governor, affirming their fidelity to the British sovereign. The signers from Frederick Township were Henry Antes, George Hubner, and Philip Leydich. Antes, who knew the Germans of Pennsylvania better than any other living man, even though they would not adopt his more advanced views, felt keenly the injustice of the accusation and the cowardice of the attack upon the honor of this faithful people, who, by reason of their alien language and social disadvantages, were almost defenceless. To vindicate more thoroughly his countrymen, he wrote a letter to Richard Peters, Secretary of the Province, making suggestions, viz :

To Mr. RICHARD PETERS, Secretary:

Sir—we have considered further concerning our address to his Honor, Robert Hunter Morris. That as there is a great number of Germans all over ye Province of Pennsylvania, which might perhaps not have heard nor indentet anything, neither of the late accusation against the said Nation in general, and may be less of our late address to his Honor ye Governor concerting ye same, and for ye more satisfaction to them all which is ignorant in it, we thought it proper to put it in public print, both in English and Dutch; if his Honor ye Governor has not already put the copy to the presse, and therefore hope his Honor will not take it amiss: because it only to that Intent that our Protestant country people might see all our reason and motive to our actions; Especially in ye Dutch colony we Intent to make a short introduction to shew them both our concern as also to remind them of their Loyal duty to the Crown of Great Britain, as likewise his Honor's answer to ye s'd address, of which I send you by this ye copy to correct; pray do not take it amiss, as you have been present you are most able to add where I have omitted, and alter where I might not have used the very same expressions his Honor made to the said address. I should have nothing against it if his Honor ye Governor should see his own ansr as much as I could remember thereof, before it is put to print and correct himself what he pleases thereof, and so send it back to Mr. Kepely, in Philadelphia, who is desired to forward ye same to print. And with this I remain with many salutations,

Sir, your Humble servant,
HENRY ANTES.

Frederick Township, December ye 24th, 1754.

Thus we see his care that all the people should know of the efforts made to preserve the harmony in the Province. And it was by this consideration of their feelings, and this confidence in their intelligence and public spirit that he retained their respect and confidence all the days of his life. He was a father to them, and in their troubles never failed to be their wise friend and courageous helper.

Chapter XIX.

Death and Burial of Antes.

HENRY ANTES' last public efforts were in the service of his fellow Germans, trying to clear them of all unjust imputation, and explaining the real sincerity of their desires for the prosperity of the Province. Then the results of his overwork and exposure in pioneer labors began to manifest themselves in the failure of his physical strength, and he went to his bed to suffer until the day of release should come. He had not many months to wait, but these were months which sorely tried his faith. It seemed as if all his desires had been denied him, although worldly prosperity and family blessings had been granted him. The Unity movement had utterly failed,—all the sects drew off from it,—it merged into the Moravian establishment, and now that had gone back to sacerdotal forms. The Educational movement had failed, for the Germans still seriously mistrusted the English, and would not submit to their forms of speech. The Germans were harrassed by all kinds of legal quibbles, and were almost defenseless in the possession of their rights. Zinzendorf, whom Antes loved so dearly, was being terribly maligned, and his cause spoken against, even by Antes' former friend, Andrew Frey, and the gloomiest of war clouds were hanging over the colony of Pennsylvania, and particularly over his beloved friends on the North Eastern frontier.

In the Summer of 1755 came Braddock's defeat, and as a consequence, a general mistrust of the Indians all along the frontier. It was along parts of this frontier that Antes had spent many years of labor and pleasant associations. In these cabins were many whom he had known and loved, and now instead of the prevalence of the peace for which he had given his life, the awful cruelty and butchery of aroused savagedom seemed to threaten to rapidly descend. The Moravians at Bethlehem were not insensible to the danger, and began to fortify their strongholds, and so far as they could, prepare for the storm. "Colonel William Franklin with a regiment of five hundred men proceeded to the Lehigh and superintended a line of fortifications. The precautionary measures were wisely taken; the line of the frontier from the Delaware Water Gap to the Potomac was the scene of burning settlements, massacre, and cruelty."

In the Forks of the Delaware, at Easton, in the latter part of 1756 great councils were held with the Indians, two years later in the same place other councils were held in which not only the Delaware Indians, but the Six Tribes or Nations sent their chiefs, to amicably settle their affairs with the people of the colony.

It was on the morning of July 20th 1755 while these troubles were brewing, that Henry Antes died, and by noon of the same day, and just after the Express sent by the Governor to General Shirley at Albany, N. Y., with intelligence of the defeat of Braddock, had passed through, the sad news was proclaimed in Bethlehem. His death awakened general sorrow, and from busy Germantown to the frontier he became the subject of eulogistic comment. The grief of the Moravians was deep and profound, for although his latter days were passed in retirement from their community, they still held him as one of themselves, and his children were in the most hearty fellowship with them. His children were educated in their schools, three of them being at Bethlehem at this time, one of these was John, who became a Moravian missionary to the Copts in Egypt, and an author of note on Egyptian affairs. Ann Catherine, his oldest daughter, was Superintendent of the Single Sisters and Girls at Nazareth and Bethlehem, while Anna Margaretta, his second daughter, was being educated in the school of the United Brethren in London, she having gone there with Zinzendorf in 1743.

Bishop Spangenberg sorrowed greatly over the death of his valued co-laborer, and lamented that he, instead of a noted man who had died about that time, was not buried at Bethlehem. It was twenty-five miles from Bethlehem to Antes' home, but on Monday the 21st of July, a delegation consisting of Bishop Spangenberg and wife, Revs. Abraham Reinicke, John Bechtel, Matthew Schrope, and eight others, with the three children of Antes, started to attend the funeral. Ten of these Brethren were the pall-bearers. The consolitary address was by the Bishop, while Abraham Reinicke read the beautiful burial service of the Moravians. There were six hundred persons present and services were held in both English and German, and thus amidst the unrepressed tears of relatives and friends from near and far, and in the sight of such a throng as was seldom seen in the country districts of the colony, the great and good man, Henry Antes, was laid to rest.

What a scene that was as the body of the dead saint was lowered into the tomb. His beloved friend and Bishop, aud his fellow workers in the Moravian interests standing by, weeping, probably reflecting that now in the awful dangers of war their counselor, holding the confidence of whites and Indians alike, could no more pour oil on the troubled waters, though several of the Moravian preachers possessed a very great influence with the Indians, prominent among whom was Timothy Horsefeld. There too, were the friends of his earlier days, his companions in the Unity movement, who now had no one to look to as their leader for the accomplishment of that glorious work. There too, were the people who, in their business trials, had gone to him for counsel and help out of their difficulties, and were never deceived. There too, were those who in the courts of the county had admired him in the administration of justice. There too, were the teachers and pastors of the schools just established to advance a higher and better grade of education. Ah! there they were, from Philadelphia, Germantown, Bethlehem, the Oley hills and valleys, the Whitemarsh and Skippack glades, from the borders of the Schuylkill to the banks of the Lehigh, yea, from the Delaware to the slopes of the Blue Mountains, rendering their last tribute of respect to him, whom they called "The pious layman of Frederick township."

And what eulogies were spoken in praise of him, not only by the men of his day, but by such men as Harbaugh, the Historian of the Reformed Church since that day. We will quote one utterance, which appeared in Sauer's Germantown paper in May 16th 1756. The value of this can be the more appreciated when it is known that the editor of that paper was not given to praise, but, being a man of rigid and austere religious convictions, was more disposed to speak in terms of severity of men and affairs, and in the London school movement had opposed Antes. " By this opportunity the editor cannot justly omit to state what he has heard as truth concerning Henry Antes, viz: When he had been for a long time prostrated by sickness, and he felt the end of life was near, a warm friend visited him and inquired, how he regarded his past administration of the office of justice of the peace? whether he felt easy in mind concerning this? He answered: He did not desire the office, and accepted it contrary to his own wishes, because so many desired him to accept; he walked in uprightness himself and administered justice to others to the extent of his ability; he never respected the person in passing judgment; when his friend or a rich man, yes, even a justice, was in the wrong, he helped the poor man to his rights, nor did he favor his children against a stranger, and he did not lie down to rest until he had examined his entire day's work, and had ascertained that he had performed his office as he would have men do to him; and when he erred through ignorance he made the correction directly. Therefore he felt quite at ease concerning his office of judge, and he longed only for dissolution. He died in a state of impartiality towards all men and parties. *Were such magistrates more numerous, the poor would not have cause to complain and to weep over gross injustice which they have to suffer because persons are respected.*"

His benevolence and spirit of forgiveness were manifested in his will, in which he gave £50 to the

Unitas Fratrum for the benefit of their Indian wards at Gnaden Hütten and elsewhere.

In a private burial place on his farm, about halfway between Keeler's and Falkner Swamp churches, Henry Antes was buried, and his grave marked by a tombstone of blue marble, on which is inscribed:

Hier ruhet
Heinrich Antes:
Ein Kleinod dieses Landes;
Ein redlich kühner
Handhaber der Gerechtigkeit
Und treuer Diener
Vor Welt und Gottes Lent,
Entschlief
In Freidrichs-Town den 20 Julü
1755
Seines alters 54 Jahre.

The translation of which is—

Here rests
Henry Antes:
An Ornament of this Land;
An upright, fearless
Administrator of Justice
and a faithful servant,
Before the World's and God's people, .
Fell asleep
in Frederick-Town, July 20,
1755
Aged 54 years.

THE GRAVE OF HENRY ANTES.

REV. J. H. DUBBS, of Lancaster.

A little spot on the hillside
  Is all that is now his own,
A little mound in a thicket,
  And a worn sepulchral stone;
For a century has departed,
  Since they gently laid him down
In the grave he himself had chosen,
  On his farm in Fredericktown.

His land is held by a stranger,
  And so is the ancient mill,
But the name of Henry Antes
  May be read on the tombstone still;
And 'tis writ on the Lamb's blest volume—
  As the angels know full well—
For he sought a home in the regions
  Where the saints and angels dwell.

He loved the church of his fathers,
  And over the stormy sea
He had borne as a precious treasure,
  Their faith to the land of the free;
But the flock was without a shepherd,
  And many had gone to sleep,
So he lifted his voice like a trumpet,
  To gather the scattered sheep.

He greeted the mild Moravians,
  As the servants of the Lord;

And with Zinzendorf and Boehler
   He labored in sweet accord ;
For they sought to unite the churches
   In a brotherhood of love,
By a " union in the Spirit,"
   Like that of the church above.

He stood by the side of Whitefield,
   And prayed in the German tongue,
When the clarion voice of the preacher
   O'er the hills of Frederick rung.
They knew not each other's language,
   Nor did they need it then;
For the one cried, Hallelujah!
   And the other said, Amen!

When his heart was almost broken,
   And he felt that the end was nigh,
To his farm in Frederick township,
   Henry Antes returned to die ;
And when his spirit departed
   To dwell in the land of the blest,
Ten loving Bethlehem Brethren
   Bore his corpse to its final rest.

I feel as I stand by his tombstone,
   That he did not live in vain ;
I am moved by his noble example
   To labor with might and main ;
For though our labors may vanish,
   Like clouds in the Summer sky,
The souls that are true to their Savior
   Shall reign with the saints on high.

THE LAST WILL AND TESTAMENT OF HENRY ANTES.

In the name of God, Amen. I Henry Antes of Frederick Township in the County of Philadelphia, Wheelwright. Being a little sick in body, but of sound mind and memory, I do make and declare this to be my last Will and Testament.

First, I commend my soul unto God my Saviour and Redeemer, by whose merits alone I hope to be saved and to enjoy eternal life, and my body I commit to the earth to be buried at ye discretion of my friends or executors.

Imprimis, I give—first of all unto Christina my beloved wife, all her bedding, clothing, side saddle, and my watch, and as much tea and kitchen ware as she pleases to have out of the whole   *   *
and a Room and fire place to live in, which she pleases to have in my house, or houses on my land in ye sd Township, and Twenty pounds Pennsylvania money yearly or annually during her natural life to be paid to her order, and that out of my lands and mills lying and being in Frederick Township above sd altogether during her natural life from ye time of my decease in stead of her thirds.

Second, I give fifty pounds Pennsylvania money unto Abraham Bemper and Timothy Horsefield or their succeeding committees for the furtherance of the Gospel of Jesus Christ to ye use of the Indian Brethren at Gnadenhutten or elsewhere under the care of the *Unitas Fratrum* now in Bethlehem in Pennsylvania.

Third, I give and bequeath unto my two eldest sons Frederick and William, all my plantation in the Township and County above sd, containing 175 or more acres of land with all the buildings and improvements thereon, and 76 acres of woodland out of the South East side of a tract containing 90 odd acres in Limirick Township between the lines of Henry Diringer and Joseph Bitting, with the proviso that they only pay or cause to be paid and allowed unto Christina my wife aforesd all that which I gave to her heretofore out of the same, and besides this to pay to my three eldest daughters 500 pounds money above sd, that is to say, to my daughter Cathrina 100 pounds thereof one year after my decease, and 100 pounds thereof to my daughter Margaret two years after my decease, and again 100 pounds thereof one year after my said wife's decease to aforesd daughter Cathrina, and 100 pounds thereof to my sd daughter Margareta ye year following, and 100 pounds thereof (ye residue of ye sd five hundred pounds) to my daughter Elizabeth ye year then following) ye sd Elizabeth had, or is to have the value of 100 pounds out of my estate heretofore) but in case my sd wife should not live so long until the two first payments * is made then * * the three last mentioned payments is to begin three years after my decease and so following as aforesaid.

Likewise I give unto ye sd sons Frederick and William four horses or mares ye choice of the whole, with their geers, and one sadle and two waggons, one iron harrow, and two thirds of all my husbandry and carpenter vessels and tools and two thirds of the sheep, four milch cows and ye house clock.

Item and fourthly I give and bequeath unto my son Henry all that my plantation in Hanover township   *   *   containing 156 acres of land, be it more or less, the which I had of my father, Frederick Antes, by Will and Testament, with all ye buildings thereon and twenty acres along side of ye same out of ye afore sd tract of land of 96 acres between ye sd line of ye sd Henry Diringer and Joseph Bitting with the proviso that he pays 100 pounds to my son John when he shall be 24 years old, and 50 pounds to my daughter Benigna when she shall be 24 years old. Likewise I give to this my sd son Henry, 2 horses or mares ye choice out of the rest of my stock with their geers and 2 milch cows and one third part of my sheep and one-third part of all my husbandry and carpenter tools and iron harrow and one waggon to be fixed up with ye old burned waggon tire   *   *   to be   *   *   under ye administration of my executors, until the said son Henry is 21 years old, and then to be delivered to him, and before that time ye said son is to serve his mother without any other further reward. But in case if a sum of money should be lawfully demanded on the sd 156 acres I had from my father above sd for fault of the deed within 15 years, such sd sum of money shall be equally paid between all my children, but if after 15 years then the sd Henry shall lose it alone.

Item, I give my said son John over and above what I have given to him before, 150 pounds to be paid to him when he is 21 years of age.

Item, I give unto my daughter Mary over and above what I gave to her before, 150 pounds to be paid to her when she is 21 years of age.

Item, unto my daughter Benigna   *   * 150 pounds   *   * when   *   *   21.

Item and lastly, after all my just debts are paid, all the rest of my moneys, bond notes,   *   * is to be turned into money and ye same to be put on lawful interest, and the interest arising is to be for the use of my sd wife during her life, and after, the whole to be divided between all my said children in equal parts, further, if any disputes should happen to arise, it shall be left to my trusty friends Timothy Horsefield, now in Bethlehem, and Daniel Benezet and Samuel Powell, in the city of Philadelphia, or to any two thereof and their judgment shall be allowed in all cases.

I do appoint my sd wife, my eldest son Frederick, and my son William to be my whole and sole

Executors and Adolph Mayer of Scipatt, and Daniel Bishope of Bethlehem to be guardians over all my children under age.

In witness whereof I have hereunto set my hand and seal this twentieth day of July, 1754.

HENRY ANTES.

Signed and sealed in the presence of
    CONRAD DODDERER,
    GEORGE HÜBNER,
    JOST BITTING.

I Henry Antes—do this 8th day of July *Anno Dom* one thousand seven hundred fifty-five make and publish this my codecil to my last Will and Testament, that is to say, concerning ye land belonging to me in North Carolina I do impower and desire my Executors to sell and dispose of the same unto the people called *Unitas Fratrum* and if they dislike, then to any person as will pay for the same.

HENRY H. A. ANTES.
his mark

In presence of
    CONRAD DODDERER,
    GEORGE HÜBNER,
    JOST BITTING.

The seal used by the testator had engraved upon it a monogram, of the capital letters H. A. in script, interwoven, and surrounded by ornamental flourishes.

INVENTORY

Of the personal estate of Henry Antes, late of the Township of Frederick and County of Philadelphia, Esqr. Deceased.

	£.	s.	d.
Cash and wearing apparell,	51	0	0
Bills, bonds, notes, and boock debts,	927	12	9
Watch,	5	0	0
Riding horse and saddle,	10	0	0
Desch, boock case and boocks,	6	0	0
Five beds and bed steads,	8	0	0
50 bushels wheat at 43, 6 pr bu.,	11	5	0
35 bu rye @ 4 s pr bu.,	7	0	0
A cobbart,	1	5	0
Three tables,	1	5	0
One chest,	0	10	0
17 chairs,	1	0	0
2 looking glasses,	0	10	0
3 iron potts,	1	10	0
Coffee mill and teakettle,	0	9	0
5 pewter dishes,	1	5	0
4 pewter basins, 27 tankarts, 13 plats and 15 spoons,	1	11	0
A small copper kettle and 2 brass skillets,	0	16	0
Earthen ware and 4 candle sticks,	0	10	0
A stilliard,	0	12	0
2 latles, 1 skimmer, 2 flesh forks,	0	4	0
2 pair of tongs, 2 fire shovels,	0	10	0
1 chaving dish and gritt iron,	0	6	0
Cloack,	7	0	0
4 spinning wheels,	0	10	0
A large Bible,	1	0	0

4 weeding hoes, 1 grooping hoe, 1 pick, 3 shovels, 2 spades, and 1 cleaver,	1	0	0
Wheelwright and carpenter tools,	20	0	0
Wheat and rye in the stran,	30	0	0
Wind mill,	1	0	0
3 pitch forks, 3 donge forks, 2 donge hooks,	0	6	0
8 hogs,	5	0	0
Apple mill,	1	10	0
Cutting box, 2 riddles, 2 half bushels,	0	15	0
Geers for four horses,	2	10	0
2 brass kettles, 3 frying pans,	3	0	0
An old gun,	0	5	0
7 milch cows,	21	0	0
6 calfs,	4	10	0
6 heifers,	11	0	0
6 steers,	13	0	0
An old brown horse,	2	0	0
A bay horse,	8	0	0
A black horse,	6	0	0
A black mare,	5	0	0
A black cold,	5	0	0
A black mare cold,	6	0	0
A gray mare,	10	0	0
A servant girls time,	5	0	0
21 sheeps,	6	0	0
	£1214	6	9

Taken and appraised this twentieth day of September *Anno Domino* 1755 by us.

         WM. DEWEES,
         GEORGE HÜBNER,
Endorsed: JOST BITTING.
  Exhibited 12th August 1756.

Chapter XX.

Henry Melchior Muhlenberg.

IN a description of this great man, and in his own record of his entrance into this country we have a picture which will suggest to us a tolerably correct understanding of the times and the people.

Prof. M. L. Stoever says of him :—" In stature Dr. Muhlenberg was of medium height, thick set, and somewhat stooped. His frame was robust, his complexion florid, temperament sanguine, with a mixture of phlegmatic—his eye bright, and expressive of a kind heart—his countenance friendly and engaging, indicative of the warm feelings of his soul—his voice was full, penetrating, and melodious—his elocution clear and effective. His personal appearance and manner were altogether such as to produce the conviction that he realized the responsibility of the position which he sustained ; his whole aspect was becoming to the holy office with which he was invested. He was a man of clear, vigorous intellect, and of varied and extensive learning. He was distinguished for the versatility of his powers, and the range of his acquirement. His mind, naturally capacious, had been subjected to the most careful culture, and the most rigid discipline; and in all his efforts he was regular, systematic and industrious. His memory was retentive, his perceptions quick, his judgments acute, and his knowledge of character wonderful. As a linguist he occupied a very high rank. He was an accurate and finished Hebrew and Greek scholar. The German, English, Dutch, French, Bohemian, and Swedish, it is said, he wrote with fluency. He could also speak in all the different languages then spoken on the continent. With the Latin he was as familiar as with his own vernacular tongue. At the meeting of Synod in 1750, we find him delivering a Latin address to the brethren in the ministry; also, at a subsequent convention, the exercises were introduced with a congratulatory discourse in Latin by a Swedish Lutherian minister, to which Dr. Muhlenberg replied in the same language. He had likewise devoted considerable attention to the natural sciences. He was very much interested in the study of chemistry, and had given some time to the study of medicine, which he found useful to him during his pastoral labors in his visitations to the poor. He was a fine musician, and performed with much skill on the organ, the harp, guitar, and the violin. He also had a pleasant voice, and it is said, sang most delightfully."

This quotation from his diary and letters is from Rev. Dr. Germann's work: "On Thursday, the

25th of November, 1742, at eight o'clock in the morning, we arrived at the town of Philadelphia. Thus far has the good Lord helped me with his kindness, grace and mercy, and borne with me, a poor sinner to the 32d year, with much patience, long-suffering and forbearance for Christ's sake. I was a stranger in Philadelphia, and knew not which way to turn. On the way had heard by chance, that the apothecary Zwieller, who was formerly in Ebenger (Georgia), now lived in Philadelphia and had connected himself with the Moravian Brethren. First I stopped at an English inn and inquired for Mr. Zwieller. He received me kindly, and when I asked respecting the German Lutherans, he informed me that the most intelligent and the majority followed Count Zinzendorf and the remainder had taken an old minister named Johann Valentine Kraft, who came hither from Germany, from Zweibrucken, where he was dismissed. Then endeavoured to hire a lodging room but could find none except in the English house in which Mr. Zwieller resided. From here returned to the English innkeeper with whom I stopped first, and inquired where New Hanover and New Providence were located. He did not know, and brought in a German from the country, who was just then in town, but who lived in New Hanover. The man's name was Philip Brandt, and he said we might ask a long time in vain, because New Providence was known by the name of Trappe, and New Hanover by the name of Falkner Schwamm. Mr. Brandt informed me that the congregation in New Hanover had engaged as pastor a man named Schmidt, who appeared to be a quack and a dentist. He said further New Hanover was thirty-six English miles distant, and that he must this evening start on his return home although the roads were in bad condition. I was still weak and swollen from the sea voyage, but not wishing to lose time resolved to accompany him, and had my effects brought from the vessel to the rented room. Mr. Brandt in the meantime hired a horse for my use and in the evening we rode quietly out of town. We fed the horses ten miles out of town at a tavern kept by a German. At the tavern sat several Germans who mentioned in conversation with each other, that the old clergyman, Valentine Kraft, had been chosen pastor in Philadelphia, Germantown and New Hanover. We remained here for the night.

"Friday, the 26th of November, we continued our journey in company with several Germans; made slow progress, as we could only walk our horses on account of the heavy roads. It was evening when we came to the two creeks, Skippack and the Perkiome, which we had to cross. The first was low, the other high. My companion rode ahead. I was to follow. My horse was light and weak, and the stream being violent he was carried down with the current a distance of several rods. He nevertheless made his way diagonally across the stream and brought me up on the other side and safely out of danger. '*Credo Providentiam,*' old Pastor Sommer (at Schorlitz Anhalt) was in the habit of often saying: My soul, forget it not! I was soaked with water up to my chest and had still ten miles to ride in the darkness to reach New Hanover, which gave me a catarrhal fever; reached under God's gracious providence Brandt's home, where I stopped over night and was hospitably entertained.

"Saturday, November 27th, at an early hour rode with Brandt further up to visit a congregation and requested him to call a meeting of the other deacons and the present elders of the congregation, in order that certain information might be communicated to them. In the afternoon two deacons and four elders met. I caused the letter of the Reverend Court Chaplain Ziegenhagen to be read to them by Mr. Brandt They said, in part, that they had indeed re-engaged the above-mentioned Schmidt to be their minister. They would, however, receive me also, and on their part respect the letter of the Court Chaplain if the members of the congregation approved. But as regarded the union of Philadelphia, New Providence and New Hanover, it seemed to them impossible for one minister to serve the three places, because Philadelphia and

New Hanover were located thirty six miles apart; secondly, in the Winter season the roads were difficult; thirdly, two streams had to be crossed. Others thought it would be well if I could arrange with old Pastor Kraft, of Philadelphia, that he should serve Philadelphia and Germantown, and I New Hanover and Providence: or that I should preach below and Kraft above. Answer: I had no assignment to Germantown, and dared not omit any of the three places until they discharge me. They thought it unfortunate that the Philadelphians, Germantownians, and Providence people had become so far committed to Pastor Kraft. I allowed the matter to rest until further advised, of his designs, and desired, God willing, to preach in their church on the 28th of November, to wit, the first Sunday in Advent, and that they should notify the aforesaid Mr. Schmidt accordingly. Hereupon the conference closed with prayer and I remained at the deacon's house. In private conversation learned that this congregation is much disturbed and divided. 'A portion sympathize with preacher Schmidt; others had separated themselves on his account; still others had previously withdrawn and wished to have nothing to do with churches and ministers; several joined Count Zinzendorf's new institution; many believed nothing whatever.' Poor encouragement!

"On the appointed first Sunday in Advent came

THE FIRST LUTHERAN CHURCH IN AMERICA

several persons to the deacon's house in which I lodged, and dealt with a Jew whose shop was here. He became engaged in a violent quarrel with a carpenter who was a member of the congregation, which was to be carried by law suit before a magistrate. They accepted, however, after much persuasion, my mediation, and became reconciled to each other, solely out of respect for me, as they said. Afterwards admonished the Jew concerning some aggravating remarks and improper expressions. He made light of my words and said I did not yet understand this part of the country. At nine o'clock rode with the deacon to the church, which a year ago was erected of squared logs, but whose interior was not completed. Men and women came on horseback to church. The preacher Schmidt also came, and sat beside me. I informed him that I purposed to-day preaching my introductory sermon, and that I would relieve him. He expressed himself courteously and said he would not interfere with me. This first sermon was on 2 Cor. V. 19, 20, 'God was in Christ, and reconciled us to Himself—be ye reconciled to God,' and was to me affecting for the reason that one year ago about this time I delivered my farewell sermon at Grosshennersdorf. After the sermon caused the call and instructions of the Reverend Ziegenhagen to be read to the meeting because the deacons and elders so desired, and rode home with the deacon. Afternoon had several visits from the congregation and opportunity to speak a good word, and to hear various opinions expressed, namely: Some were pleased with the prospect because they hoped the congregation would in time be placed under good discipline; those who sided with preacher Schmidt were not fully satisfied, and thought he should not be entirely discarded, even though he was not ordained, and now and then indulged in a little too much drink; even among the best are none without fault; he might at least be deputy, and be allowed to preach when the new minister was compelled to be absent. Others who had severed their connection long ago, said they wanted to see how the matter turned out, inasmuch as they had been hoodwinked before, and no one could tell whether I myself had not written the letter. Finally, some halted because the call fixed the salary at forty pounds sterling a year, which might prove a tax and a burden upon their children and grandchildren, and preferred to have nothing to do with the matter. I secretly rejoiced that God's foresight had kept back the tenderly beloved servant Boltzius (at Ebenezer, Georgia), and had spared him the knowledge of this heart-sickening state of things. On the sea voyage I suffered physically nauseating sea-sickness, and now I must endure a moral emetic and learn to know its healing effects.

"Monday, the 29th day of November, three elders of the congregation accompanied me nine miles down to New Providence, for the purpose of conferring with the deacons there, and stopped with the widow Schrack, whose husband, a deacon, and one of those who often petitioned the Rev. Mr. Ziegenhagen for a minister, died the past Summer. We therefore sent for the eldest deacon yet living. I showed him the Court Chaplain's letter. He recognized immediately the Court Chaplain's signature, and he expressed pleasure at my coming. They had indeed abandoned the hope and no longer expected anyone, because they had received no answer to their last letter of 1739, and therefore a year ago made a request to the Reverend Consistory of Darmstead for a minister. A short time since an old clergyman named Valentine Kraft had arrived, who said he was sent by the Consistory. He had, it is true, brought no credentials, but he stated that they would follow. Besides there were persons who knew him as a minister in Germany. He (the deacon) made the suggestion that I should confer with Mr. Kraft and either take charge of the two lower congregations in the town, or the two upper in the country. I allowed the matter to rest for further examination.

"Monday, the 30th of November, the eldest deacon of the Trappe rode with me to the younger, and from there to Philadelphia, where we arrived, wearied, at nine o'clock in the evening. I was compelled on account of my hired horse to stop again at an English inn. The landlord conducted me into a large room, where, as he remarked, gentlemen of position sat. Immediately upon my entrance they asked me whether I was a Moravian, Lutheran, Presbyterian, or Established Church minister? Answer: They should learn better manners than to accost a stranger with such questions. They excused themselves. Afterwards paid for the hired horse and went to my lodging room.

"On Saturday, the 11th of December, 1742, I quitted my rented room, and considering my other expenses, had to pay the Englishman dearly. At nine o'clock in the forenoon I rode with Mr. Kraft out of the city, through Germantown, at which place my patron led me before several houses and exhibited me to the people as a curiosity. During the afternoon we had continuous, heavy rains, became thoroughly wet, and were compelled to cross the two swollen streams Schippack and Perkiome in the darkness of the night. One of the deacons, who resided on this side of the streams, kindly accompanied us through the water, so that preserved by God's care, we reached the home of the oldest deacon in Providence, and spent the night with him.

"On Sunday, the 12th of December I preached for the first time in Providence; doing so in the deacon's barn, the people here having, as yet, no church building. After the sermon Mr. Kraft laid before the assemblage the letter of the Court Chaplain Ziegenhagen, and the members appeared pleased therewith. Mr. Kraft did his best to induce me to remove from the city and to recommend the congregation to my favor. In this vicinity dwell several persons who are natives of the Grand Duchy of Hesse Darmstadt and who had in youth good instruction. In the evening several visited us, with whom we had edifying conversation.

"On Monday, Dec. 13th, Mr. Kraft rode ahead on horseback to New Hanover. Towards evening I was also taken there. Mr. Kraft had in the meantime stopped with a deacon and had held counsel with the matron of the household on the questions: Whether it would not be well that I should marry? Whether I should take in marriage a city lady, or a farmer's daughter from the country? Out of the abundance of the heart the mouth speaketh! The old man is determined by main force to make me happy, in soul and body, in this world. I lodged with Mr. Kraft at the oldest deacon's. In the evening we were favored with the company of a mountebank who was summoned to the neighborhood to question a dead man, who allowed himself to be frequently seen and who terrified the people. I admonished the man to desist from such sinful imposture and from causing ignorant persons to commit sin. He refused to yield, however, because his personal gain was involved. Another asked me, 'What is the sin against the Holy Ghost?' I answered from the twelfth chapter of Matthew as fully as time would permit.

"On Tuesday, December 14th, I was requested to baptize a child of the congregation. Mr. Kraft accompanied me and ordered how it should be done. The elders, deacons, and a number of members, had in the meantime assembled. Mr. Kraft left me alone in the room and went out to the assemblage and began to address them as follows: 'I have now brought you a new minister, and will give him to you in preference to all others; make provision without delay that he may remain and live with you. I will unite another congregation eight miles farther up, with this as a charge. If you do not at once make preparation and accept the favor thankfully, I will take him immediately to Lancaster and install him there as pastor.' Upon this arose confusion and excitement in the gathering and several of the elders and deacons came in to me and asked, 'What does this mean?' 'Whether the old man was my superior?' 'Whether the letter from the Court Chaplain was not genuine?' I could now shield Mr. Kraft no longer, but read to the meeting, in his presence, once more my appointment and pointed out that I was assigned to Philadelphia,

Providence, and New Hanover, and asked whether they all agreed thereto. All answered Aye! aye! I further told them that I had no connection with Mr. Kraft, and that he had no authority over me except such as he improperly assumed, or such as they gave him. He could not install me in Lancaster or any other place. He endeavored to excuse himself and bring himself again into favor, but without avail; the people were glad and the elders took me in charge. Visited a man, who heretofore, on account of the disorder, refused to connect himself with the congregation, but who now, in expectation of improvement, intended to unite with it. The man had a small hut alongside his dwelling house, in which I could study and sleep, but could not walk; this they gave me for my abode. It was somewhat more roomy than the cabin in the sloop on which I came from Charleston, or the tub of Diogenes.

"The elders were of the opinion that I could properly abandon Philadelphia on account of distant location; I told them, however, that it was not left to my option to surrender one or the other of the three congregations without the approval of my superiors, or until they themselves released me. They prayed that I would in the beginning remain part of the time with them, inasmuch as a party during my absence since the first sermon had notified their old minister Schmidt to preach again.

To this he replied that he would do so provided they brought him written permission from me. I promised to remain until next Sunday, and, God willing to preach here.

"After I had inspected my dwelling place, returned to the deacon's house, where Mr. Kraft still remained, and said to him in private that he had committed a serious offense; this was not the way to bring our Evangelical Lutheran religion into prosperity. On Wednesday, the 15th, Mr. Kraft withdrew, having played his role, and traveled towards Lancaster. I had various visitors among them of those who were wise in their own estimation and desired to engage in disputation. Thursday, the 16th, I took possession of my appointed abiding place, and thanked God for the privilege of seclusion, and for the opportunity of collecting thoughts undisturbed. Friday, the 17th, was visited by a man who spoke to me concerning his soul's condition, who evinced a fine knowledge of the articles of our faith and who was deeply moved, as in conclusion, we joined in prayer. In the evening gave a little instruction to the children. Saturday, 18th, devoted to meditation; had also visits from several persons, who made charges against their neighbors, and wished me to allude to and condemn these matters in my sermon to-morrow. Answer: This is not Christ's teaching, Matthew 18: 15-17, 21, 22, tell us our duty. It is said, also, admonish thy friend, it may be he hath not done it, Ecclesiastes 19: 13, 14, 15.

"On Sunday, December 19th, I preached here upon the gospel for the fourth Sunday in Advent to a large concourse of people from the vicinity; after the sermon baptized the children in the presence of the congregation, and explained the meaning of baptism, because certain people oppose baptism, especially of children; reminded also the old of their covenant of baptism, and announced that on Christmas, Providence permitting, divine service would again be held. The two deacons from Providence were present, and had brought with them a horse for me. As soon as service was concluded here, I hastened with the deacons to Providence, and found a numerous assemblage in and around the barn, to whom I explained the lesson of the epistle for the day, which was listened to with emotion and devoutness. In the evening had an encouraging meeting with several persons at the deacon's house. The people were hungry for the word of God, and felt delight in conversation concerning their soul's salvation.

"On Monday, Dec. 20th, a deacon came from Hanover for the purpose of taking me back, but I could not go with him; for according to Mr. Kraft's direction I was expected in my first sermon in Philadelphia, to announce that at Christmas the Lord's supper would be celebrated here. But owing to the turn in affairs at Hanover, I was compelled to return to Philadelphia and explain the reason of my inability to be in Philadelphia on Christmas day. Tuesday, 21st, I traveled with the oldest deacon from Providence to the city and safely reached it in the evening. Friday, 24th, during last night a violent rain set in, which still continues. I promised to come to Hanover to-day. The Providence people furnished me with a strong horse, which carried me safely on my journey; but I was compelled to remain over night this side of Hanover, on account of the rise in the water.

"On Saturday, the 25th of December, namely, the first day of Christmas, I rode to the church and held service with a largely attended congregation, the two deacons from Providence being among those present. In the evening the elders and deacons of both congregations met and subscribed a certificate as follows: 'We, the elders and deacons of the Protestant Lutheran congregations at New Hanover, Providence and Philadelphia, do testify and affirm by subscription, that we have accepted with a thankful heart the Rev. Melchior Muhlenberg as a lawful called, ordained and by our supplications sent and represented minister of the gospel, by the Rev. Frederick Michael Ziegenhagen, His Majesty's German Chaplain and member of the Society for promoting Christian knowledge; and promise to furnish our minister with the necessaries required for his living in the lawful vocation, and to assist him in every good disposition and direction, which he gives for our and our children's spiritual welfare, etc.: Dec. 25th, 1742.' Signed by the deacons and elders of the respective churches.

"On the 26th of December, the second day of Christmas, I rode, in company with the deacons to Providence, where I found a large meeting, and preached to them upon the gospel of the day. We held service in the barn, but not without great inconvenience on account of the raw winds. There was again a large attendance of all sorts. Afterwards rode with Mr. Marstellar over the two creeks and remained with him during the night.

"On the 27th of December, started off early alone; had twenty-one miles to the city, and bad roads; fed my horse on the way, and reached town at one o'clock P. M.

Chapter XXI.

Gottlieb Mittleberger's Book.

THE description of a visit to Pennsylvania in 1750-54, translated by Henry S. Dotterer, with prefatory remarks: "In the year 1756, Gottlieb Friderich Jenisch issued from his press in Stuttgart, a small book, entitled: 'Gottlieb Mittleberger's journey to Pennsylvania in the year 1750 and his return to Germany in 1754; containing a description of the country in its present condition, as well as a detailed account of the unfortunate and pitiable circumstances of most of the Germans who have settled in that land and are moving thither.' It is from this book the following passages are taken.

"It will be seen that Mittleberger, brought from Heilbronn, in Wurtemberg, the organ for St. Michael's Lutheran Church, Philadelphia, and during his stay here the organs for the churches of the same denomination at Trappe, New Hanover and Lancaster were brought over. He arrived at Philadelphia in the ship Osgood, William Wilkie, master, last from Cowes. The male adult passengers to the number of 138, representing 480 souls, signed the delaration of obedience to the laws, on the 29th of September, 1750. Among these was Gottlieb Mittleberger. It does not appear that he came with the intention of remaining in the country. While here he took occasion to examine closely the condition of the German immigrants. The results of his observations were, as a whole unfavorable to the infant State. While he saw much in the extent, fertility and salubriousness of Pennsylvania to commend, his judgment told him the German was much better off under the oppressions of the Fatherland than under the hardships to be encountered in the new world. The descendents of the sixth and seventh generations of those brave and hardy emigrants know how mistaken he was. The hundreds of thousands of Americans who trace their ancestry to these strong men will smile at the earnest notes of warning he sounded against undertaking the adventurous journey. He was sincere. He could not foresee the tremendous future of this country. What has come to pass was then beyond the power of man to know. 'He moves in a mysterious way his wonders to perform.'

"Mittleberger was a close observer. He noted particularly the characteristics of the country, the people and the customs which differed from those of his native land. He touched upon those matters of greatest interest to the intending emigrants, and furnished a faithful portraiture of the condition of the new-comers here. At that time this Abendland was to the people of Germany a wonderland. The distance, measured by time and the perils of travel, was vastly greater then between the two continents than now.

"Mittleberger's book has a value of another sort. He brings us face to face with the customs and circumstances of those early times—stern realities which have now from lapse of time and the lack of records come to be invested with somewhat the romance of unreality. Not only this: our author took the precaution to question the old men of his day, who had come over in infancy with the earliest emigrants, and to note their graphic descriptions of the really primitive times. This volume is found in two places in Philadelphia; one copy on the shelves of a public library, the other in the hands of a private collector of rare books. How many more may be extant, it would be interesting to know. Certainly, the book must have had some circulation in Pennsylvania; and the reasonable inference is that copies may have been brought over by emigrants. It would seem that none of our historians have thus far met with this interesting publication. By none of the writers of Pennsylvania German history is it mentioned. The poet Pennypacker, however, in 'The Old Trappe Church,' has immortalized in verse 'Gottlieb, colonial musician,' and 'the sounds of his low melodies.'

"The work is also preserved in Wurtemberg, although copies are rarely found. It is quoted by Professor Hartmann, and F. Mayer in answer to the question ' Who brought the first organ to America?' exultingly answering 'He was good Swabian, the the organist and school-master Gottlieb Mittleberger, of Enzweihingen, and the organ was built in Heilbronn. The work is dedicated to his Highness, Prince Charles of Wurtemburg, who read the book in manuscript, and it found his princely favor. Mittleberger says: I started in the month of May, 1750, from Enzweihingen, in the district of Vaihingen and my birth-place, for Heilbronn, where a completed organ was awaiting shipment to Pennsylvania. With this instrument in charge I took the usual route, sailing down the Neckar and the Rhine to Rotterdam in Holland. At Rotterdam I embarked in a vessel carrying about 400 souls—Wurtembergers, Durlachers, Palatines, Swiss, etc.—which crossed the North Sea to Cowes, in England, and, after a nine days stoppage here, proceeded across the great ocean. On the 10th of October, 1750, I landed at Philadelphia, the capital of Pennsylvania. From my home to Rotterdam occupied seven weeks, including the detention there—the unusual length of time was owing to the numerous stops on the Rhine—from Rotterdam to Philadelphia the sea journey consumed fifteen weeks. I was nearly four years in the country, and, as my letter of recommendation shows, held the position of organist and schoolmaster in the German Augustus Church in Providence township, and gave private instructions in music and the German language at the house of Captain Von Diemer, as the following certificate states:

"Whereas the Bearer, Mr. Mittleberger, Musick Master, has resolved to return from this Province to his native Land, which is in y Duckdom of Wirtenberg in high Germany: I have at his Request granted these Lines to certify that y above nam'd Mr. Mittleberger has behaved himself honestly, diligently, and faithfully in y Offices of Schoolmaster and Organist: during y Space of three years: in y Township of New Providence, County of Philadelphia and Province of Pennsylvania, &c. So that I and all his employers were entirely satisfied and would willingly have him to remain with us. But as his call obliges him to proceed on his long journey: we would recommend y s'd Mr. Mittleberger to all Persons of Dignity and character; and beg their assistance, so that he may pass and repass until he arrives at his Respective Abode; which may God grant, and may y Benediction of Heaven accompany him in his journey. Deus benedicat surceptis ejus und ferat cum ad amicos suos maxima prosperitate Dabam, Providentiæ Philadelphiæ

Commitatu Pennsylvania in America die 25 Apr.
A. D. 1754. JOHN DIEMER, CAP.
SAM. KENNEDY, M. D.
T HENRY PAWLING, ESQ.
HENRY MARSTELLER.
MATTHIAS GMELIN.

"I made myself carefully acquainted with the state of the country, and what I have written is partly my own experience, and partly gathered from trustworthy persons in a position to know whereof they speak. I could, indeed, have related much more had it occurred to me that I should ever be called upon to publish anything regarding Pennsylvania; for which task I did not consider myself well fitted. Only the misfortunes which I myself endured upon my journey thither and hither (for in that country itself I fared well, having readily obtained a good livelihood and having gotten along well) and the wicked devices which the Newlanders tried to play upon me and my family, as I shall hereafter relate, awakened in me a sense of duty not to conceal that which I knew.

"The most important object of this little work was the miserable and distressful condition of those who migrate from Germany to this new land, and the inexcusable and remorseless dealings of the Dutch traffickers in human beings and their manstealing emissaries, the so-called Newlanders, for they entrap, as it were, the people of Germany, by means of all sorts of plausible deceptions, and deliver them in the hands of the great Dutch sellers of souls. The latter derive a large, and the Newlanders a small profit from this trade. This, I say, is the principal reason for the publication of this book. I am bound by a vow to the performance of this duty. For before I left Pennsyvania, as it became known that I intended to return to Wurtemberg, many Wurtembergers, Durlachers and Palatines, of whom many are there, who every day of their lives bemoan and bewail their lot in having left their Fatherland, besought me with tears and upraised hands, for God's sake, to make known to Germany their misery and heart pangs, so that not only the common people but also the princes and nobility, might know their experience, and that innocent souls might no more be persuaded by the Newlanders to leave the Fatherland and be led into a life of slavery.

"The journey takes from the beginning of May to the end of October, an entire year, and is attended with hardships impossible to describe. The reason is the Rhine boats from Heilbronn to Holland have to pass by thirty-six customs towns, at all of which an examination was made at the convenience of the customs officers. By this means the boats and their passengers are detained a long time, compelling the emigrants to spend a great deal of money. Thus the passage on the Rhine is made to consume four, five, or six weeks. When the passengers at last reach Holland they are again detained four, five to six weeks. As everything is very dear here, the poor emigrants are forced to spend nearly all their means. They are liable to many sad accidents here. I saw with my own eyes a man lose two children by drowning, as he was embarking with his family at Rotterdam. The ships in making the passage from Holland to Cowes in England, when met with contrary winds, often take two, three or four weeks, but with favorable winds the passage is made in eight days or less. Here a thorough examination is made and the customs dues are collected, and it sometimes happens that here the ship lies at anchor, eight, ten or fourteen days, or even longer, until she is fully loaded. During this time every one must spend of his little remaining money and provisions, which he intended to take with him for the sea voyage, so that most persons afterwards, upon the wide ocean, when they need comforts more, suffer the pangs of hunger and want: many, indeed, often find themselves in great need already on the passage between Holland and England. When, finally, the ship in Old England, at the city of Cowes, raises anchor for the long voyage, the misery actually begins. For it often takes from eight to twelve weeks to make the voyage to Philadelphia when unfavorable winds are encountered; when, however, the winds are favorable, it only takes seven weeks. During the voyage a deplorable condition of things exists on board—stench, mould, vomiting, diseases incident to the sea, fevers, diarrhœa, headache, costiveness, scurvy, cancer, soreness of the gums, and the like, all of which are caused by the strongly salted food and meat, and by the foul and dirty water, of which many become wretchedly sick and die. There is also lack of the necessaries of life, and hunger, thirst, chills, fever, dampness, fears, need, quarreling; and lamentation, besides other miseries; for example, want of cleanliness. The misery reaches its highest pitch when there is a storm of two or three days and nights duration, when every one fears the ship and all its passengers will go to the bottom. In such a situation the people utter shrieks and prayers in dire confusion.

"In a storm the sea rages and foams; sometimes the waves roll mountain high, and sometimes they dash upon the ship as though to sink it; the ship is beaten every moment by the storm and waves from one side to the other, so that it is impossible either to walk, sit or lie, and the closely packed passengers in their berths are thrown together in a confused mass, the well with the sick. It can readily be imagined that such hardships, which none had looked for, necessarily debilitate many beyond their power to endure, I myself suffered a severe illness on the sea, and know very well what feelings I experienced. The wretched people are often in great fear, and I frequently engaged with such in singing, prayer and comforting words, thereby consoling them, and when it was possible, and the wind and the waves permitted, held an hour of prayer with them on deck; and I baptised five children in cases of extremity because we had no ordained clergymen aboard. I also held service every Sabbath by reading a sermon, and at the giving to the waves of the dead commended to the good Lord the souls of the dead and the living.

"Among the well persons, the spirit of discontent becomes so strong and irrepressible that one will call down curses upon the others, or upon himself, or upon the day he was born, and sometimes they are almost ready to destroy each other, want and hunger both urging them, they deceive and rob each other. One blames the other of being the cause of undertaking the voyage. Oftentimes the children reproach their parents, the husband will blame the wife, and brothers and sisters, friends and acquaintances will threaten vengeance against each other; but most of all against the man-stealers. Many a one sobs and cries: 'Oh, if I were but once more at home, even though compelled to lie down with the cattle in their pens!' Another calls, 'Oh, good Lord, if I had but once more a morsel of good bread, or a drop of good fresh water!' Many persons moan, and sob, and shriek for their homes most pitifully; in addition to this most of them feel the pangs of homesickness. In the midst of so much misery naturally many sicken and die; and must be cast into the sea, and their connections, or those who induced them to make the voyage, frequently attempt to follow them in their despair. It is almost impossible to console such grief-stricken persons. In a word the sobs, shrieks and wailings continue day and night in the ship, causing the heart of the most hardened man who hears them to bleed. Sometimes the father dies upon the voyage, leaving wife and children; sometimes the mother, leaving little children; or perhaps both parents, leaving little children; and often whole families, one after another, so that the dead lie in the berths beside the living; especially is this the case when infectious diseases rage in the ship.

"That the majority of the passengers become sick is not to be wondered at, when we state that, with all these afflictions and miseries, cooked meals are served but three times a week, and very poor and very scant at that. These eatables are not relishable owing to their uncleanness, and the water supplied on the ship is often black, and thick, and full of worms, so that one cannot swallow it without aversion although burning with thirst. Ah, truly! on the sea one would often pay a large sum of money for a piece of good bread, or a drink of good water, to say nothing of a drink of good wine, were it possible to obtain them. I had to experience such sufferings sufficiently. Sea water it is impossible to use, because it is salty and bitter as gall. If this were not so, the voyage could be made with much less cost and without incurring so many hardships.

"Finally, when, after the wearisome and perilous voyage, the vessel nears the land, which the passengers have desired so anxiously and so longingly to see, all crawl upon the ship's deck to gaze upon it in the distance. When they discern the shores, they weep for joy, and pray, and sing to the good Lord in love, gratitude, and praise. The sight of the green earth gives the people on the vessel new life, even to the sick and half dead, making their spirits to leap and shout with gladness. They are willing to bear patiently all their miseries in the hope of soon landing in safety. But alas! when the ship after the long voyage, arrives at Philadelphia, no one is permitted to leave her, except such as can pay their passage money or can furnish good sureties; those who have not the means with which to pay must remain on board until they are sold and are released from the ship by their purchasers. Now, the condition of the sick is the most serious, for the healthy are more readily and consequently more willingly purchased. The suffering sick oftentimes remain in the ship, lying in the harbor two to three weeks, sometimes even dying. Many such, if able to pay their indebtedness, and permitted to leave the ship promptly, might have saved their lives.

"The traffic in human beings at the ship market is conducted as follows: Every day Englishmen, Hollanders and high Germans from the city of Philadelphia, and from other places, sometimes from a distance of twenty, thirty or forty leagues, come to the newly arrived ship, which has brought passengers from Europe and has them for sale; and select from the healthy persons those suited to their wants, and bargain with them as to the length of time they are willing to serve in payment of their sea passage, which usually they owe in full. When an agreement is reached, it happens that grown persons bind themselves in writing to serve for three, four, or five years, according to their strength and years, for their passage money. The quite young, from ten to fifteen years of age, must serve until they are twenty-one years old. Many parents trade and sell their own children like cattle, by which means only the parents, if the children assume the payment of the passage money, are released from the ship. As the parents do not know to what sort of persons or to what place their children will go, it often happens that parents do not see their children for many years after their departure from the ship, or it may even happen they will not again see each other during life. The wife must be responsible for her husband if sick, and likewise the husband becomes responsible for his sick wife, and assumes the passage money, and must serve not alone for himself, but also for his sick wife for a period of five to six years. But if both are prostrated by illness, they are taken from the ship to the Hospital, not, however, before it is found impossible to find a purchaser. As soon as they recover they must serve for their fare, or, if they have property pay therefor. Often it happens, that the entire family—husband wife and children—become separated, by reason of having been bought by different persons; this being the case when such persons can pay nothing whatever on account of their passage.

"Work and business in this new and wild country are hard and various, and many a one, who has but recently come in, is compelled to work hard, in his old age, for his bread. Of young persons I will say nothing. The principal occupations consist of cutting wood, felling oak trees, and pulling up and out, root and branch, large tracts of forest, 'to clear,' as it is there called. These forest lands are, after this turning upside down, divided into fields and meadows. From the best of the hewn wood, are made fences around the new fields, for all meadows, grass fields, fruit orchards and grain fields are enclosed and protected by timber rails made of thick split wood, laid one upon the other zig zag. In these enclosures the horned cattle, horses and sheep, are put out to pasture. Our Europeans, who are sold into service, must work hard, for new fields are constantly made, and in this way they find, indeed, that oak stumps stand as firmly in America as in Germany. I will relate the sad case of a Wurtemberger. In the fall of the year 1853, Bailiff Daser of Nagold, who was known to us, arrived at Philadelphia with his wife and eight children, under unfortunate circumstances. For there was stolen from him on the passage property of the value of eighteen hundred florins, and in consequence he became involved in a great law suit with the English ship captain at Philadelphia, by which he gained nothing, but had to pay heavy costs besides. Mr. Daser was to pay six hundred florins for passage for himself and family. But as he had been robbed of his money, all his moveable property including chests, were sold at a vendue for a mere trifle, in consequence of which he and his wife were thrown into still greater distress. As he was about to borrow money to purchase a plantation, he was also deceived by the lender. He had agreed with the lender to return the borrowed money in two years, but the person who drew up the obligation, or bond, as it is here called, inserted, at the instigation of the conscienceless lender, instead of two years, *two days*.

"Mr. Daser signed this, not knowing that he

was bringing misfortune upon himself, for he did not understand English. Because he did not return the money in two days, everything he had was sold, and even taken from his person (*N. B.*— He had not even received the money, having allowed the time—two days—to elapse through his own incautiousness and because of all kinds of deception on the part of the lender). Yes, he would even have been cast into prison, or would have to sell his children, if he had not been through my intercession, rescued by Captain Diemer, who has at all times cared for the Germans. Captain Diemer, after this, through compassion furnished him food, money, beds and a home, until the law suit was ended, and made kindly intercession, by reason of which Mr. Daser was saved from being placed in the Debtors' Prison. At my departure Captain Diemer promised Mr. Daser and me, giving us his hand upon it, that while he lived he would in future help the Daser family to procure their bit of bread. Mr. Daser was eight weeks a guest at our table, and slept with me; he has, however, in truth, become low-spirited and weak in mind by the many sad trials through which he has passed. His two eldest unmarried daughters and his eldest son, were shortly before my departure, compelled to bind themselves to service, in writing, each one for a term of three years. Every year while I was there, from twenty to twenty-four vessels with immigrants arrived at Philadelphia, making in four years an aggregate of over 25,000 souls, not including those who died on the sea or other portion of the journey, and excluding those vessels which sailed with immigrants to other English colonies, such as New York, Boston, Maryland, New Scotland, and Carolina. In consequence of the numerous arrivals the colonies filled up, and human beings became of very small value in specie in the city of Philadelphia. That, in spite of this, so many citizens move to America and in particular to Pennsylvania, is owing to the swindles and deceptions of the socalled Newlanders. These man stealers deceive persons of all conditions and professions, among them soldiers, scholars, artisans and mechanics. They lead astray the people of princes and the gentry, and hand them over for sale at Rotterdam and Amsterdam. They receive from the merchants for each person of ten years or older three florins or one ducat; on the other hand, the merchants received for one person at Philadelphia sixty, seventy or eighty florins, varying according to the debt incurred by the passenger on the voyage. When a Newlander has gathered a ship load of passengers, and it does not suit him to go to America, he will stay behind and spend the Winter in Holland or elsewhere. The following Spring he will again take the money of the merchants, travel about and announce that he has come from Pennsylvania for the purpose of purchasing all sorts of wares and leading emigrants thither. Frequently the Newlanders state that they have authority from their countrymen or the magistrates there, to collect inheritances, and that they are willing by this safe and convenient opportunity to take with them their friends, kinspeople or even father or mother; and it often happens that aged people follow them in the hope, as they were made to believe would be the case, of being better cared for.

"In Pennsylvania and in other English colonies the Newlanders who go to Europe are often entrusted with many letters. When they reach Holland they allow the letters to be opened, or they open them themselves, and (the painful truth must be written) the letter is copied falsely, or perhaps thrown away. I have heard one of these thieves relate in Pennsylvania, that in Holland plenty of persons, and certainly Jews, could be found, who, for a very little money, would engrave seals and imitate handwriting perfectly, as desired. They are so expert in copying every stroke and letter, mark and characteristic, that the person whose handwriting has been imitated, would admit that it was his own. By such acts they deceive persons who are far from credulous, and accomplish their wicked purposes the more surely.

"I must here mention a matter omitted at the proper place. The forenoon following the anchoring before Philadelphia of a ship with a load of immigrants, all the males above the age of fifteen are taken out of the vessel, taken in a boat to the wharf, landed, and marched two by two to the Court House or City Hall. Here they must swear allegiance to the Crown of Great Britain. When this is done, they are again taken back to the ship. After this only, the trade in human beings begin, as described. I have merely to add this, that in purchasing, the persons asks neither for certificate nor good name. If one had escaped the rope and had it still around his neck, or if he had left both his ears in Europe, it would be no obstacle in his way in Pennsylvania. If, however, he allowed himself to commit excesses here, there is no escape. For gallous and wheel-deserving people Pennsylvania is therefore a desirable place.

"Philadelphia is the capitol of Pennsylvania, in which commerce is carried on; and is quite large, handsomely built according to a plan, with broad streets and numerous cross streets. All the houses are built of stone or brick, and are raised as high as four stories, and they are roofed with cedar shingles. It takes a day to go around the city, and every year three hundred new houses are erected. It is believed in time it will become one of the largest cities in the world. The principal language and the common law is English. There is neither wall nor rampart, being deemed unnecessary. On both sides are navigable waters—on the East the Delaware, and on the West the river Schuylkill—which unite below the city. There is a newly built splendid Court House or City Hall, with four doors and four entrances. It is one hundred feet long and one hundred feet wide, stands in an open place, and has on the four sides large English plate windows. In this city are already eight churches, three English, three German, one Swedish, and one Quaker.

"Greater freedom exists here than in other English colonies, and sects of every belief are tolerated. You meet here Lutherans, Reformed, Catholics, Quakers, Mennonites, Herrenhuter or Moravian Brethren, Seventh Day Baptists, Dunkers, Presbyterians, the New Born, Free Masons, Separatists, Free Thinkers, Negroes and Indians. Still the Evangelical and Reformed compose the greater number. Of the unbaptized persons and who do not desire baptism, there are many hundred souls; many pray neither morning nor evening, neither before or after meals. Among such people will be found no religious books, much less the Bible. In one house may be found a family whose members believe in four, five or six different creeds.

"In Pennsylvania there is no profession or occupation regulated by law; every man can deal in, or carry on what he will, or can. If any one wishes, or is able to do so, he may conduct ten different professions, and no one dare prevent him. And if, for instance, a youth in half a year acquires a knowledge of his art or trade, he can pass for a master and he may marry when he chooses. It is remarkable that the young people, who were born in this new country, are very quick to learn, apt and skillful; for many a one, after examining a fine piece of work will make one like it, while in Germany it would take a man several years to learn to make a perfect one. Here also are many farmers capable of making many ingenious articles in a short time. When these young people have attended school for half a year they can generally read any book put before them.

Pennsylvania is a healthy country, has mostly fertile soil, good air and water, many mountains, and much even land; it is thickly wooded, and where not inhabited is an unbroken forest through which many large streams flow. The soil is very productive and grains of all kinds yield abundantly. It is already populous, inhabited far and wide, and in it several new towns have been founded, viz: Philadelphia, Germantown, Lancaster, Rittingstaun (Reading), Bethlehem and New Frankfort. Many churches have also been built in the country, but many persons have from two to ten leagues to go to church. Every one, male and female, goes to church on horseback, even if the distance is but half a league. This also is the custom at weddings and funerals. At weddings and funerals in the country as many as three to five hundred persons on horseback may be counted.

"I will describe more in detail the burial custom. When a person dies in the country, where the habitations are widely separated by the plantations and woodlands, the time appointed for the burial is announced to the four nearest neighbors only, and they in turn notify their next neighbors. In this manner the funeral notice in twenty-four hours travels over a circuit of more than fifty English miles. If possible, at least one person from every house attends the funeral at the appointed time, coming on horseback. While the people are assembling a slice of sweet-cake is handed to those present, and a cup of warm West India rum containing lemon, sugar and juniper berries, which are highly esteemed there. After this a drink of the juice of fruit, made warm and sweet is handed around. The custom at a burial in America is similar to that at a wedding in Europe. When the people have all assembled, and the time for the burial has come, the corpse is carried to the general burying ground, or, if that is too far off, the body is buried, perhaps in a field of the farm of the deceased; and those assembled all ride in silence after the coffin; sometimes as many as one, two, three, four, to five hundred persons on horseback may be counted. The coffin is made of fine walnut and varnished. The coffins of persons of means are ornamented with handsomely wrought brass handles by which they are lifted and borne to the grave. When the deceased is a youth four maidens bear him to the grave; on the contrary a deceased maiden is bourn by four unmarried associates.

"It is in that country not uncommon to hear quite uneducated men preach in the open air, for the sectarians hold that the learned of the present time are not Apostles, and that they make their learning a mere trade. On the other hand there are in Pennsylvania many earnest ministers, who have by the grace of God and by untiring effort brought many to the christian belief; I can bear witness that our Evangelicals (Lutherans) have baptized and confirmed many grown persons, both white and black. On such occasions a great multitude come together. There are in Pennsylvania many worthy English, Swedish, Hollandish and German ministers. I am well acquainted with the following: Among the English, the three brothers Dennent (Tennant) and Mr. Datt. Three Swedish who have with our ministers a very close union, having annually a joint conference. The German Evangelical Lutheran ministers are: Rev. Mr. Muhlenberg, Senior, at Providence and New Hanover, Mr. Brunholz, in Philadelphia, Mr. Handschuh, in Germantown, Mr. Kurz, in Tulpehocken, Mr. Wagner, in Readingstown, Mr. Heinzelman, in Philadelphia, Mr. Schulz, Mr. Weygand, Mr.

Schwenk, Mr. Schartel, at the Blue Mountains, Mr. Hartwick, in New York, Mr. Gorock, at Lancaster. The Reformed are: Mr. Schlatter, Mr. Steiner, Mr. Siebele, Mr. Weiss, Mr. Michael, Mr. Streitter, and Mr. Laidig, besides the Dutch and others whose names are not known to me.

"No ministers in Pennsylvania are entitled to any stipend or titles; they receive only what is contributed by their church members during the year, which is very uncertain and variable; some heads of families give according to their means and pleasure, yearly, two, three, four to six florins, many however give very little. At infant christenings, funerals, and marriages the pastor usually receives a thaler. The clergy are not furnished free dwelling-houses or other similar advantages. They receive many gifts from their catechumens. The same applies to the schoolmasters. Since the year 1754 England and Holland give a large sum of money, yearly, to support six English Reformed churches and as many English free schools for the general use of the many poor in Pennsylvania. Many hundred children, on account of the great distance and many forests, are unable to attend the schools. Owing to this many of the planters lead quite a barbarous and heathenish life; for as it is with the schools, so it is with the churches, because usually the churches and schoolhouses are erected at the place where most of the neighbors or church members reside. The pastors in Pennsylvania have no power to punish any one, or to compel any one to attend church, nor have they any authority to correct one another because they are not subject to any higher authority. The minister is hired by the year as are the herdsmen in Germany, and when he does not preach to their liking, his services will be dispensed with, and one who will please them will take his place. It is, for this reason, very difficult to be an upright minister; the more so as he has to suffer and to contend with much from the many opposing and in part Godless sects. The most exemplary ministers are often, especially in the country, ridiculed, abused and mocked to their faces, like Jews. I would therefore rather perform the meanest herd service in Europe than be a minister in Pennsylvania. Such unheard of coarseness and wickedness are the result of the excessive liberty in the land, and the blind zeal of the sects. To many in Pennsylvania the freedom they enjoy is more harm than good both in body and in soul. There is a saying: 'Pennsylvania is the farmers' heaven, the mechanics Paradise, and the officials' and ministers' pandemonium.'

"The drinks in Pennsylvania are many. First, excellent and healthful water; second, a mixture of milk and three parts water; third, good apple cider; fourth, small beer; fifth, delicious English and strong, sweet beer; sixth, a so-called punch, made of three parts water and one part West India rum (if rum cannot be had, whiskey is taken, rum, however, is far preferable) mixed with sugar and lemon juice; seventh, Sangaree, which is still more choice, and is made of one part Spanish wine, with sugar and nutmeg; and eighth, German and Spanish wines are to be had in plenty in all drinking houses, the last named costing a reichs thaler per quart. The mixed drinks are served in porcelain vessels, called bowls, formed like a soup dish.

"All professions and trades have plenty to do; no beggars are seen, for each district maintains and cares for its poor. In the country the people live a considerable distance from each other, often from a mile to a mile and a half from their nearest neighbors. The reason of this is, many proprietors hold fifty, or a hundred, or even as many as four hundred acres, divided into orchards, meadows, farm land, and woodland. A plantation of this size, usually has ten, fifteen or twenty acres of orchard, and from the fruit grown large quantities of cider and whiskey are made.

"Peach and cherry trees are planted by many landholders all along the avenues from one plantation to another and they produce in abundance. One kind of peach is red inside and outside, as large as a lemon, but round and smooth, and ripens about St. Bartholomew's Day. There are also yellow, red-streaked, and green peaches. Still another species named the cling stone, is sweet when ripe; these are, when not quite matured, pickled like cucumbers. Pears, on the contrary, are scarce; plums do not succeed, being often injured by mildew. Each planter keeps his cattle, horses and sheep in pastures upon his own premises, or allows them to run at large in the thickets, and evening and morning the cows are brought home to be milked and then allowed to run at large again. In this way the live stock sustains itself, saving the labor of feeding them daily, as in Germany; and during the entire Summer not one is put into a stable, except when a cow is about to drop a calf; frequently, however, search is made in the woods, and old and young are found together; or, the cow with the calf comes unexpectedly to the house. For this reason, also, there is not needed in all the Province a sheep or cattle herdsman, the stock being turned either into the enclosed fields or into the woods where there is plenty of pasture and in many places much goes to waste.

"In Pennsylvania, as indeed all of over North America, from Acadia to Mexico, grow wild black and white grapes, which grow up on oak trees and other supports. Many grape vines are at the ground as thick as a tree, and often hang so full of grapes that the branches of the tree bend under their weight. When blossoming they have a strong odor, and in October they ripen. Little wine is made, however, because much sugar is required. Many grapes are taken to Philadelphia to market. It would much improve these grapes if they were trimmed as in Europe, but as the inhabitants here live so far apart, and the numerous game and birds waylay the grape plant all the time, it is not likely much wine will be made.

"Sassafras trees, which are not found in Europe, are very numerous here. An effective tea for colds is made of the blossoms; the wood and root of this tree is also used as medicine. Some of these trees are of the thickness of a man's body; the leaves look and smell like laurel leaves; the flowers, however, are a golden yellow, like the primrose but much smaller. I gathered and took with me a package of sassafras blossoms, which proved to be my best medicine on the voyage. Sugar maple trees are also found in great numbers; these are as thick and as high as oaks. In the spring of the the year, when they are in full sap, the sugar water can be tapped, have tried this myself in March, when the sap began to flow; cutting into a tree near the ground through the bark and inserting the tube of a quill, through which the maple water flows, as when whiskey is clarified. In a quarter of an hour I had a glassful of sugar water. The people here, who gather the maple water, fill a kettle with it, let the water boil until it is thick, and when cooled it is a thick honey. The sugar maple trees stand generally beside the water brooks in the forests and grow wild. The beautiful tulip trees grow here abundantly. In the month of May when they blossom they are covered with tulips, colored flaming yellow and red, and almost as natural as those which grow upon the ground. The trees are as thick and as high as the largest cherry trees. I have seen another tulip tree in bloom which is cultivated in gardens; these, however, are not larger than the dwarf fruit trees; They bloom in August, having white and red flowers. The former and larger tulip trees do not bloom until twenty or more years old. In America are found entirely different kinds and species of trees, flowers and herbs, as well as grains. For example, the common and slightly regarded daisy is as scarce in Pennsylvania as the finest and rarest flowers are in Europe, so that it is grown as a choice flower in their gardens. Equally rare there is the juniper plant, which is valued more highly than the rosemary with us, and the juniper berries are sold at a higher price than pepper corn. Juniper bushes are also planted in the gardens there. All other European flowers and shrubs are equally scarce. That which is little esteemed in Germany is dear and scarce, and, on the contrary, that which is not regarded as valuable here is costly in Germany. The Germans who have settled here grieve for the good things they have lost, especially do the Wurtembergers and Rhinelanders miss their excellent wines.

"Walnut trees grow in indescribable quantities. This fine coffee-brown hard wood is valuable and useful. Much of it is sawn and exported to Holland, England, Ireland, and other countries, where it brings high prices. These walnut trees bear, yearly, nuts, the size of ordinary apples, which yield oil. They have bark and leaves like our nut trees. Indian or wild cherry trees are not frequently seen; I have however eaten Indian cherries from these trees, but did not find them palatable like the European. The grandest ornaments of the forests are the beautiful and useful cedar trees, they grow mostly upon the mountains. Their wood has agreeable odor, has little sap, and particularly for organ pipes is exceedingly valuable, for the pipes made of this wood are of finer and clearer tone than those of tin, of which fact I have seen ample proof. The houses in Philadelphia are roofed entirely with cedar shingles. A roof of this wood, when a heavy rain falls, rattles like a copper or brass roof.

"In this country no May-beatles are seen; on the other hand, every five years a terrible army of insects named Lockis (Locust) makes its appearance. They are somewhat larger than the May-beatles and are capable of inflicting great injury upon the crops in the fields and upon the forests. Red and white snails are not found here, and the frogs have entirely different notes; they do not croak, but they bark, and this barking begins as early as March.

"In America are found birds of species quite different from those of Europe. Those entirely similar to the European are crows, swallows, and the diminutive hedge sparrow. The American birds are formed in wondrous beauty, and their brilliant plumage and delightful singing cannot be sufficiently extolled. 1st, there is a yellow bird with black wings; 2nd, red with black wings; 3rd, entirely yellow; 4th, the starling, larger than ours, quite blue with red wings; 5th, vermillion, with a tuft upon the head; 6th, entirely blue; 7th, white with black wings; 8th, vari-colored; 9th, green with a red head; 10th, a species, black, white, and spotted, which can imitate the song and whistle of all birds; this bird can mock successfully more than thirty birds in half an hour. There is another bird there which the whole Summer day calls out distinctly 'mach doch fort,' 'mach doch fort.' Another, heard mostly in the night' calls: 'whip-poor-will,' 'whip-poor-will,' and is called by this name. In Pennsylvania are found no storks, no cuckoos, no larks, no yellow hammers, no nightengales, no quail, no finches, no canary birds, no black birds, no red breasts, no vineyard favorites, no sparrows.

"The most remarkable, not only in Pennsylvania but in the whole world, is a little bird which is seen very rarely. It is not as large as a May-beetle, but rather the size of a gold beetle. It glitters like gold, varying green, blue and red. Its bill is somewhat long and sharp pointed as a needle, and its legs like fine wire. It feeds only on the honey of the flowers, and is for this reason sometimes called the sugar bird. It builds its nest among the flowering plants in the garden; its nest is not larger than a cupping glass, yet four or five young are usually found in it. Its wings move with indescribable rapidity, and make a whizzing noise. When not flying it may usually be heard singing subtily and charmingly; that is, if fortunately it is possible to get in close proximity to one. I will not venture to state at how large a price this little bird is sometimes sold to the wealthy. But they do not live long, because it is impossible to give them suitable food.

"In Pennsylvania are found during the Summer season many species of snakes and other reptiles; especially is this the case in the Blue Mountains, where many snakes of ten, twelve, fifteen to eighteen feet in length have been seen; and persons and cattle have often been fatally bitten by these frightful and dangerous creatures. They are white and black, green, gray, and black with yellow stripes. Of all these the rattlesnakes are the largest and most terrible; yet the blacksnakes are by actual measure twelve to fifteen feet long, and as thick as a man's arm, and the more obnoxious because of their marvelous powers to charm, and this they do simply by their gaze, under which all that comes before them, be it a rabbit, a bird, or squirrel, must descend from the tree and approach the snakes, when they, at last, draw it to themselves and devour it. They can also climb the highest oak and other trees, and have the power to charm little children so that they cannot move. When children are heard to shriek in horror, it often happens, when rescued that large snakes are found lying before them. Some rattlesnakes are larger than the foregoing species; they have been found eighteen feet long and as thick as a maple tree. This species has on the end of its tail rattles, which rattle so that they may be heard at a distance. They rattle only when they are angry or when they see some one. Every year a rattle is added to the tail. These snakes have scales like fish, black, blue and green, presenting the appearance of mother of pearl. It has happened to persons who live in the forest, that snakes have entered their houses and have crept into their bedding upon which these persons slept at night. These persons when they had lain some time upon their beds, became too heavy for the snakes, who then became restless and were driven out of the house and killed.

"In Pennsylvania there is a pretty sight, in the night, during the Summer, when myriads of fire bugs fly in the air, giving the appearance of a fall of snow of fire. A few years since a newly arrived German was thrown into great terror of these insects. He had not been told about them, and had never before seen them. He was working late in the evening in the field, when several fire bugs flew to and fro about him, which terrified simple Hans so much that he left his work and ran with all speed to his house. When, overcome with fear, he reach his family, he said, frightened and trembling: 'Oh, Lord, preserve me! How many fiery spirits hover about in this country! Oh, dear Lord, if I were only once more in Germany.'

"The savages, or Indians, who have intercourse with the English are very numerous, living beyond the Ohio, and beyond the Hudson, upon which Albany is situated: thus on both sides—to the right and to the left of Pennsylvania. Both these rivers are large and are about three hundred miles distant from Philadelphia. These savages live in huts in the forests, beyond these waters, and so far beyond that it has been found impossible to find the farthest limits of their habitations. The farther into the interior one goes the more savages are seen. They sustain themselves in various ways; some shoot game, others dig roots, others also grow tobacco, and Indian corn, which they eat raw or boiled; they trade in deer hides, beaver skins and valuable fur skins.

"The savages which live on the borders of the European settlements are frequently seen and some of them speak some English. I have several times seen entire families, and had, on one occasion, the opportunity, at the suggestion of Captain Diemer, to play the organ for a savage family, at which they became quite merry, manifesting their surprise and pleasure with motions of genuflections. Those Indians who wander about among the whites, instead of clothing wear blankets, such as are used to cover horses, wrapping them about their naked bodies. They have nothing upon their heads or feet. Their bodily formation does not differ from ours, except that their skins are a dark yellow, which, however, is not their natural color, for they besmear and toast themselves. At birth they are as white as we are. The men and women have long and smooth hair; the men do not wear a beard, and if in youth the beard begins to grow they pull out the hair, and they have, like the women, smooth faces. Owing to the lack of beard and to the similarity of the clothing worn, there is no difference is the appearance of the men and of the women. When these savages wish to beautify themselves, they paint their foreheads and cheeks red, and hang a large ornament from their ears.

"Every Fall they come in great numbers to the city of Philadelphia, bringing with them a variety of small baskets which they make cleverly and neatly, skins of wild animals and desirable furs. Besides this, when they have all assembled they will sell a tract of more than a thousand acres of land, which is still forest, to the Governor. Many presents are given to them in the name of the country and the city, such as blankets, guns, rum, whiskey, and the like, whereupon they become merry, especially when they become drunk, with their own most strange orgies. Some of them are very strong, stalwart and courageous. They address everybody in their own language, even the Governor, and they walk with the fleetness of a deer. When spoken to concerning the ever true God, the Creator of Heaven and Earth, they do not understand it, and return only this reply: They believe this, there are two beings; one good, the other evil; the good made everything that is good, and the evil everything that is bad; therefore it is not necessary to pray to the good for he will do no evil, but the evil one must be prayed to so that he will do no harm.

"Of the resurrection of the dead, salvation, heaven or hell, they know nothing. Their dead they bury where they die. I have been told by truthful persons that the savages slay their aged people and bury them, when by reason of advanced years they are unable to move about, or fall by the way. When, however, a savage takes the life of another person, when not in battle or on account of old age, be the murdered man of our or their people, he must die. They lead the malefactor before their Indian King for trial, from there back to the place where he committed the deed, slay him on the spot, bury him at once, and cover his grave with wood and stones.

"When the savage people come to the city of Philadelphia, and here see the handsome and sumptuous residences, they are amazed and they laugh at the Europeans for expending so much pains and money upon their houses, and say: 'This is quite unnecessary, one can live without such houses;' especially are they astonished at the European costumes and the costly adornments.

"When two savages give themselves in marriage, the bridegroom at the betrothal places upon the bride a piece of a stag's foot, meaning thereby that he will feed his future wife with meat; his bride gives him an ear of Indian corn, indicating thereby that she will provide bread for her beloved husband and children. They care for each other, and remain together until death separates them. Old Indians have frequently been asked concerning their origin, to which they answered: They knew nothing and can say nothing but that their most remote forefathers lived in this wilderness and that it is not right that the Europeans take their lands from them. In consequence of this they must constantly move farther back into the wilderness for the means of sustenance.

"The wonderful weapon of these wild people is simply a bent bow, in the middle of which in front they lay a sharp and pointed cut stone as long as a finger; at the rear, this stone is an inch in width, and on both sides as sharp as a knife. They aim accurately, and when they have shot an animal, and it does not fall, they follow it until they capture it, for they can move with the speed of a horse. I have as evidence brought with me a stone of the kind with which the Indians or savages have shot game. This was their only weapon before they obtained guns from the Europeans. It is, too, interesting to hear the Indians sometimes complain, that, since the Europeans have come into the country, they are visited by frequent snows, intense cold and tornadoes, and awful, heavy thunder storms, which before were unknown. This may or may not be true; but the Indians ascribe these occurrences to the Europeans, and for the reason that they, and principally the Germans, are most terrible blasphemers.

"Rev. Mr. Schartel, who was formerly pastor at Zell and Altbach in the Duchy of Wurtemberg, but who is now stationed as pastor in the township of Macungie at the Blue Mountains, in Pennsylvania, sixty odd miles from Philadelphia, made a remarkable discovery. In 1753, while seeking a path out of the wilderness, having lost his way, he found on a hillock surrounded by a growth of trees, a stone doorframe, which was planted in the ground. At first he thought it a work of nature, but when he rubbed off the moss, with which it was overgrown, and examined it carefully, he found on the upper cross stone a Hebrew sentence engraved, containing the following words: 'To this place did the God of Joshua keep us.'

"When in this Province a couple desires to be united in marriage, in opposition to the wishes of the parents and relatives on one or both sides, the couple rides off on one horse. Inasmuch as the lady has more privileges than the gentleman, he must sit behind his beloved on the horse. In this position they ride to a justice and say to him: We have stolen each other; pray unite us in marriage. When this has been done, no one, not even parents or friends, can throw any further hindrance in their way.

"In Pennsylvania a man might travel a year without spending a Kreutzer, for it is customary, in this country, when a man with a horse comes to a house to ask the travellers: Will you have something to eat? Then some cold meat, which remained over at a previous meal, is set before the stranger. To this is added white bread, butter or cheese and plenty to drink. If the traveller wishes to remain over night, he and his horse are kept free of charge. If one enters a house at meal time, he is immediately invited to sit up to the table and partake of what is spread. There are, however, also inns, at which can be obtained whatever is desired.

"The English ladies in Pennsylvania and the other English colonies have the same rights and privileges as the ladies of Old England. They are uncommonly handsome and well formed, generally gay in spirits, affable, very free in manner, spirited, shrewd, and skillful, but withal very proud; they carry themselves in great state and expect much attendance from gentlemen. The English gentlemen indulge them accordingly and hold them in high respect. A man dare not undertake to marry a woman unless he is able to maintain her without requiring her to work, otherwise she will make him unhappy or possibly leave, for no housework can be required of her except that which she is willing to do. They delight in visiting or going into company, whether it is agreeable to the husband or not. I would rather strike three men of the English than tap one woman. If a man strikes his wife, and he makes complaint to a neighbor's wife his life is no longer safe. If this occurs a number of times, he will have to take to his heels, as she may put him in prison a long time, or possibly to the gallows. She cannot be compelled to take back her husband. That the English ladies are in general handsome is not to be wondered at, when we consider that from childhood their wishes are indulged, they take no coarse food or drink, they are not allowed to do work, and rarely go into the sunshine. The evidence of an English woman is accepted in court in preference to that of three men. It is said that they acquired these privileges as far back as the time of Queen Elizabeth.

"In the Blue Mountains several rich ores have been found, which have been as much as possible kept secret; they consist, however, for the most part of copper, brimstone and iron, which yield rich returns. Several iron works and glass houses are in operation; and large quantities of cast iron and glass work are shipped from this Province to Ireland, England, Holland, and to the other colonies. In Pennsylvania, at a place well known to me, has been found a quarry of the very finest blue, white, and red marble, from which the English make handsome altars, drawing rooms and columns. Four book printers have already established themselves in Pennsylvania, namely, in Philadelphia, two—one English, the other German; the third in Germantown, and the fourth in Lancaster. A number of grist, saw, oil, fulling, powder and paper mills are in operation; also tanneries and potteries, and lime and brick kilns. There are German and English apothecaries in Philadephia; indeed, no trade or occupation can be named that is not to be met with in the city or in this new country. Even the travelling glaziers and the scissors grinders have begun to make their rounds, who, to the English people, seem very odd and laughable. Nothing is wanting in this country more than wine production, as before stated; but in time, I have no doubt, this will be carried on.

"In Pennsylvania and the remaining English colonies are numberless negroes or blacks, who are doomed to serve as slaves all their lives. The price paid for a strong, industrious, half-grown negro is two, three, to three hundred and fifty florins. These black people marry after the English manner.

"I have met several persons who came, some seventy-five years ago, as children with the first immigrants. These have related how in the beginning things looked in this country, and how much misery they endured. It is easy to believe that the original settlers in this new and wild land suffered many hardships, for these few people must on account of the many surrounding Indians, have felt great fear. Nearly all employment was lacking; their seedings they had to hoe in on account of the dearth of horses and cattle; moreover, they had for many years after their arrival, to do without grist mills, and having to crush and grind the grain or kernels upon broad stones; bread baking evidently was then poorly done. Worse than all, for a long time no salt was to be had. Wood and meat was plentiful, for they shot all kinds of game, when powder was not wanting. For a long time a number of persons would own a single horse, until horses and cattle were imported from other countries. On account of there existing great number of large and small wild animals, snakes and vermin, they lived continually in fear and apprehension; for this reason, they had to keep going, day and night, around their huts, blazing fires to keep off bears, panthers and wolves, at present, however, bears and panthers are rarely seen in Pennsylvania.

"Indeed, several years ago, a large bear came to Captain Diemer's place, in the night, climbed upon an apple tree and commenced to shake down apples just like a human being, upon which the dogs were aroused. The bear, however, paid no attention to them, and continued to shake down the apples. Finally, the master of the house, being made acquainted with the matter by the servants, at once proceded, armed with two rifles, and accompanied by the farm hands and dogs, to the orchard, and when he came near enough to the apple shaker to see him clearly in the moonlight, he gave him his compliments with a bullet; upon which the wounded bear raged furiously and tumbled head over heels from the tree to the ground. As the beast was about to escape, the Captain shot again, upon which it made another somersault, and a third bullet incapacitated it. The dogs were put upon it, and they finally choked it. This affair called forth great rejoicing among the neighbors.

"The first and second days of May in Pennsylvania are devoted to a general jubilee, in which, principally, the unmarried people of both sexes take part. All amuse themselves in games, dancing, shooting, hunting, and the like. Those of the young people who are natives of that country, decorate their head coverings with a piece of the fur of a wild beast, and with it a picture of the wild beast, preferred by the wearer. Thus distinguished the young fellows walk about the city calling out, hurrah! hurrah! None dare place upon their hats these emblems unless they are born in this country, and they are called Indians.

"In Pennsylvania there is among all, in high or low condition, in city and country, this custom: when one enters a house, or meets another, he shakes hands first with the father and mother of the family, after which he greets, in the same manner, every one else present, although the room may be filled with persons at the time. This greeting and hand shaking is practiced with strangers as well as with the most intimate acquaintances; and the address made by the English as well as the Germans, always is: 'Good friend, how do you do?' This agreeable custom is derived partly from the numerous English Quakers in

Philadelphia, and partly from the Indians themselves, who first performed this ceremony. To tell the truth, quarrels rarely occur between the people; strangers trust each other further than acquaintances do in Europe. People are also more sincere and affectionate than in Germany; from this cause our Americans live more quietly and peacefully than the Europeans, and this is the result of that freedom by which all are equal.

"Music at this time is rather rarely heard. In the principal city, Philadelphia, there is no music either in the English or German churches. Occasionally several Englishmen will conduct a concert upon a spinet or clarichord, in a private house. I brought to this country the first organ, which is now in a High German Lutheran Church. This instrument was made in Heilbronn. When it was erected and tuned, it was consecrated, with great rejoicings, to the glory, praise and worship of God by the Christian St. Michael's Church. At this great festival were present fifteen Lutheran clergymen, together with the united consistories of all the evangelical churches. The audience was a vast multitude, many persons having come as far as thirty to one hundred miles to see and hear the organ. The number of people, who were inside and outside the church, both German and English, was estimated at several thousand. On the second day of this solemn festival a conference was held by the Lutheran pastors and consistories, at which I was selected as school-master and organist. As I became more widely known in Pennsylvania, and as the people learned that I brought handsome and excellent instruments, many English and German families came a great distance to hear and to see the organ, and they expressed wonder thereat, having never before seen or heard such an instrument. There are now six organs in Pennsylvania; the first, in Philadelphia; the second, in Germantown; the third, at Providence; the fourth, at New Hanover; the fifth, at Tulpehocken, and the sixth at Lancaster, all of which were brought into the country during the four years that I remained there.

"The English mode of dress prevails in Pennsylvania, both for ladies and gentlemen. Ladies wear no hoop petticoats; yet everything they wear is fine, neat and expensive. The gown and skirt are cut from one piece and sewed; in front the gown can be parted, and under the gown the ladies generally wear a handsomely quilted skirt, trimmed with ribbons; the upper gown or skirt must reach to the shoes, and is made of cotton calico, or other rich and handsome material. The ladies always wear fine white aprons; on the shoes usually large silver buckles, around the neck a fine color, at the ears expensive pendants with precious stones, and upon the head white caps embroidered with flowers, and trimmed with lappets and laces. Their gloves are of velvet, silk or the like, and are generally trimmed with silver or gold lace, or expensively embroidered. Their neck handkerchiefs are either of velvet or of pure silk, and are likewise sumptuously embroidered. When they go visiting or ride out on horseback they wear a blue or scarlet cloak, which covers half the person. Upon the head they wear black or other handsomely colored taffeta hats instead of straw bonnets; these hats take the place of the parasol, but are much prettier. If our ladies should see these hats, they too would soon have them. When they go on horseback they carry an expensive horsewhip or karabatsche, which is strong and made of fine wire, whalebone, or the like, and is finely wrought. The handle is usually made of red velvet, plush or tortoise shell, ivory, mother of pearl, and frequently even of solid silver. These whips the ladies carry when they travel in the country, or in the city when going to church, and they keep them in the hand when in church. Many ladies ride with the best horsemen for a wager. An English maid-servant in Philadelphia is dressed as finely as a lady of quality in Germany. The English ladies are usually pretty; they wear generally false or colored hair.

"Men's wearing apparel, especially that of the English, is with the farmers as with persons of classes, quite expensive; it is made of English cloth and material of that character; and they wear fine shirts. They all wear wigs, the farmers as well as the retired persons. In Philadelphia they wear quite large and only fine hats, and no wonder seeing that this is the home of the castor and beaver. In the Summer time beaver hats are worn not turned up, especially is this the case in the country. At this season also are worn fine light coats, or only waistcoats, which are neatly made of delicate linen cloth or fustian. All gentlemen have their hair cut off short during the Summer, and wear only a cap of fine white linen, and upon this a hat not turned up. When visiting the hat only is taken off, not the cap. If one makes a journey of but three miles' length, he takes with him a long coat and a pair of boots, which are turned down half way and reach only to the middle of the calf. These precautions are taken on account of the sudden changes of the weather.

"In Pennsylvania all houses are massive and built of free stone, and are usually, when they stand separate, provided with English plate glass windows. Stoves are rarely seen in the rooms; instead all houses are supplied with French chimneys, before which all seat themselves, and drink their good English beer, and the like, or smoke their pipes of tobacco. When these chimneys are properly constructed, no smoke is noticed. Before all houses, on both sides of the door, are built benches, reaching about four feet from the house; at the front of both are posts which support a roof forming a structure somewhat like a Summer house. These benches or seats are not to be seen in the country only, but also in the city of Philadelphia before all houses. In the evening when the weather is favorable people sit upon them, or else go visiting. Owing to the sameness of the houses and the streets, one can see a great part of the city in half an hour. In the city are seven principal churches, but only one tower, which is, however, of great height and beauty. In all the city are only two small bells, and when they are rung, the people go to their several churches. The city and church authorities, joined the last year of my stay, in taking the preliminary steps towards procuring three bells of various sizes from London, in Old England. In the country none of the churches have a tower, nor are they supplied with a bell or clock; consequently to the newcomers, the evenings are very tiresome, until they become accustomed to the monotony. On the other hand, almost everybody, farmers as well as persons of leisure, carry silver watches; and these are also generally worn by the English ladies.

"On the 21st of September, 1752, the new calendar was introduced in Pennsylvania and in the other English American colonies. By this was jumped from the 11th of September to the 21st. This change was not made without much opposition, as well by members of the English church as by their sects. Especially did a number feel great solicitude because one Sunday, with its gospel, is entirely left out, and therefore is lost.

"In the Province of Pennsylvania three principal roads are laid out, all of which make their start in Philadelphia, and extend into the interior as far as it is settled; the first road leads to the right over the Delaware towards New Frankfort; the second, or middle road, leads towards Germantown, Rittingstoun (Reading) and Dulppenhocken (Tulpehocken), and extends beyond the Blue Mountains; the third leads to the left towards Lancaster and Bethlehem.

"After a nine weeks voyage, on the 10th of October, 1754, after enduring calamities, want and deadly dangers, we arrived safely at London on the Thames, on the identical day which, four years before, I stepped from the vessel in America. We all joined in heartfelt thanks to God, and kissed the earth for joy, and realized fully the force of the words of the 107th Plsam, which describes the terrors of voyagers upon the sea. To the Triune God, for this great mercy and care, be glory, praise and thanks, through time and eternity."

Chapter XXII.

The Descendents of Henry Antes.

This table may not be absolutely perfect. Such a work can only be accomplished through the co-operation of all the descendents. But this is as good and as reliable as we have been able to obtain at the present time. We have endeavored to insert only the names of those living, except in a few instances to show the line of ancestry. If any one can give us further information we will be pleased. The numbers indicate the generations starting with Henry Antes as 1. When children of the same family follow, the line of descent is only given with the oldest.

1. Ann Catherine, born November 8th, 1726. For some years she was Superintendent of the Single Sisters and Girls at Nazareth and Bethlehem. Subsequently became a resident at a Moravian settlement in Bethabara, North Carolina. She was wedded four times: to Martin Kalberlahn in July 29th, 1758; to Gottlieb Reuter; to Rev. John Casper Heinzman; to Rev. John Jacob Erust. We have not been able to obtain the names of her descendents. She was a woman of great sweetness of character and intelligence.

2. Ann Margaretta, born September 9th, 1728. In 1743 she accompanied Zinzendorf to England and completed her education in the school of the United Brethren in London. Here she met and married in 1766 Rev. Benjamin Latrobe, a Moravian minister. They had four children. The eldest, Christian Ignatius, became a minister, a traveler in South Africa and an author, some of his children became ministers, and one, a grandson, a distinguished English engineer (T. Frederick Bateman of London). The second son, Benjamin Henry, was a traveler, soldier and architect. He was the architect of the central building of the Capital at Washington, and many other prominent public buildings. The Latrobes of Baltimore are his descendents. The third son, John Frederick, became a distinguished M. D. at Dorpat in Livonia, Russia.

1, 2, 1, 2.	Peter Latrobe, Sec'y of Moravian Church in England.
4.	Rev. John Antes Latrobe Kendall, Yorkshire England.
5.	Charles Joseph Latrobe, Ex-Lieut. Gov. Melbourne, Australia.
1, 2, 2, 4.	John H. B. Latrobe, Baltimore.
5.	Julia E. Latrobe.
7.	Benj. Henry Latrobe. Ex-Chief Engineer, Baltimore & Ohio, R. R.
1, 2, 2, 4, 1.	Ferdinand C. Latrobe, Baltimore.
1, 2, 2, 4, 1, 1.	Thomas Swann Latrobe.

	2. Charlotte Fernan Latrobe.
	3. Ellen Virginia Latrobe.
1, 2, 2, 4, 3.	Richard Steuart Latrobe, Towson Baltimore county.
1, 2, 2, 4, 3, 1.	Mary Mactier Latrobe.
	2. Osmun Latrobe.
	3. Emily Mactier Latrobe.
	4. Edna Claiborne Latrobe.
1, 2, 2, 4, 4.	Virginia Cogswell, Brunswick, N. Jersey.
1, 2, 2, 4, 4, 1.	J. H. B. Latrobe Cogswell.
1, 2, 2, 4, 5.	Lydia Loring, Washington D. C.
1, 2, 2, 4, 5, 1.	Lydia Latrobe Loring.
	2. Jean Loring.
1, 2, 2, 6, 1.	Charles H. Latrobe, Baltimore.
1, 2, 2, 6, 1, 1.	Gamble Latrobe.
	2. Elise McKim.
	3. Eleanor Baynton Latrobe.
1, 2, 2, 6, 2.	B. H. Latrobe, Wilmington, Delaware.
1, 2, 2, 6, 2, 1.	Laurason Latrobe.
1, 2, 2, 6, 3.	Mary Onderdonk, College of St. James, Maryland.
1, 2, 2, 6, 3, 1.	Adrian Onderdonk.
1, 2, 2, 6, 5.	Eleanor Vinton, Boston, Mass.
1, 2, 2, 6, 5, 1.	Eleanor Vinton.
	2. Hazel Vinton.
	3. Pamela B. Vinton.
1, 2, 2, 6, 4.	Catharine Weston, Baltimore.
1, 2, 2, 6, 4, 1.	Latrobe Weston.
	2. Henry Weston.
	3. Arthur Weston.

3. Philip Frederick, born July 2d, 1730. He was three times appointed justice of the peace in

Philadelphia Co., and was an ardent patriot in the Revolution. A reward was laid on his head by the British. He was a man of rare ability and intelligence, and possessed great mechanical skill. In 1776 he and Mr. Potts at Warwick Furnace *cast the first cannon*, an eighteen pounder, cast in America. He was a member of the Provincial Council, a judge of election in Philadelphia Co., July 8th, 1776, a member of state convention of July 15th, 1776, member of the General Assembly, was colonel of Philadelphia Co. militia, was one of the persons designated to sign the issue of $200,000 paper money issued April 10th, 1777. 1779 removed to Northumberland Co., being impoverished by the war. Here he was justice, county commissioner, judge of Court of Common Pleas, member of State Assembly and county treasurer. Died in Lancaster September 20th, 1801. He left a large number of descendents by his first wife. By his second wife he had one daughter, who became the second wife of Simon Snyder, afterward Governor of Pennsylvania. His youngest son, Antes Snyder, was kidnapped, and the sensation spread all over Pennsylvania. He (Antes Snyder) graduated at West Point, became a prominent engineer, in 1860 was chief engineer of Reading Railroad. We find that among his descendents are a number of distinguished engineers.

1, 3, 2, 8, 1.   Oscar M. Dering, Columbus, Wisconsin.
1, 3, 2, 8, 1, 2. —— Campbell, Milwaukee, Wis.

1, 3, 2, 8, 1, 3. Guy V. Dering, Columbus.
1, 3, 2, 8, 2, 1. Oscar E. Dering, Texas.
             2. Addie Dering Jones.
1, 3, 2, 8, 4. Philip Frederick Dering, Darlington, Wis.
1, 3, 2, 8, 4, 1. Charles Lewis Dering.
             3. Kemper Dering.
1, 3, 2, 8, 5. Charles L. Dering, Portage, Wis.
1, 3, 2, 8, 5, 1. Jessie Giberson Dering.
             2. Toma Taylor Dering.
             3. Charles Maxwell Dering.
1, 3, 4, 2, 1. Antes Huber (deceased)—widow (Caroline) resides in Myerstown, Lebanon Co., Pa.
             5. William E. Huber.
             Mrs. Sarah A. Craig, Wymore, Sage Co., Neb., wife of Henry Antes Winther.
1, 3, 4, 1, 1, 2. Margaret R. Winther.
             5. Charles E. Winther.
             6. Anna G. Winther.
             7. Grace Winther.
1, 3, 4, 1, 2. Mary S. Winther.
1, 3, 4, 5, 2. Mrs. Elizabeth Antes Hobart, Renova, Clinton Co., Pa.
1, 3, 4, 5, 1. Hannah Susanna Hobart, married Samuel Barkenbine. She died leaving two children.
1, 3, 5, 1, 1. Grandchildren of George Snyder, Mary Josephine Snyder, born 1829.
             2. Catherine Helen Snyder.
             3. Ann Alice Snyder.
             4. Amelia Jenks Snyder.
             5. Simon Snyder.

            6. Frederick Smith Snyder.
            7. Henry W. Snyder.
            8. Charles A. V. Snyder.

1, 3, 5, 2, 1. Harriet M. Snyder App.
            2. Catherine Antes Snyder Crane.
            4. Henry F. Snyder Crane.
            5. George Snyder Crane.
            6. Ellen L. Snyder Riley.
            7. Antes Snyder.
            8. James Duncan Snyder.
            9. Jesse Duncan Snyder.
            Mrs. Mary B. Snyder, widow of 1, 3, 5, 5. Antes Snyder, Musselshell, Meagher Co., Montana.

1, 3, 5, 5, 3. Francis Snyder.
            4. Frederick Antes Snyder.
            5. Edward Melville Snyder.
            6. John Antes Latrobe Snyder.
            7. Florence Snyder.

4. William, born November 18th, 1731. William Antes was Sub-Lieutenant of Philadelphia County during the Revolutionary war, Commissioner of sequestrated estates, etc., and held other positions of responsibility during the war. After the war he was Commissioner of Northumberland county. In 1809 he was residing in Genesee county, N. Y.

1, 4, 6, 2, 1. Charles Hammond Antes, New York City.
            2. Robert Hayes Antes, Genesee, Ill.
            3. Henry T. Antes, Genesee, Ill.
            7. Katherine Marshall Antes

1, 4, 6, 3, 1. William Gibbs Antes, Canandaigua, N. Y.
1, 4, 6, 6. Abner Barlow Antes.
1, 4, 6, 6, 1. Mary Antes, Canandaigua, N. Y.
        2. Sarah Hayes Antes, married Edgar I. Warner, Obilene, Kansas.
        3. Catherine Bemis Antes, married Charles W. Chase, New York City.
        4. Eliza W. Antes, Canandaigua, N. Y.
        5. Abner Barlow Antes, Waterloo, Iowa.
1, 4, 6, 6, 3, 2. Bessie Bemis Chase.
        3. George Cotton Chase.
        4. Alice Leighton Chase.
        5. Charlotte Goldsmith Chase.
        6. Charles William Chase.
1, 4, 6, 7. Lucinda (A.) Reid, Kewanee, Ill.
1, 4, 6, 7, 2. William (A.) Reid.
        3. Elizabeth Eddy Reed.
        4. Frank Hays Reid.
        5. Anna Louisa Reed Little.
1, 4, 6, 7, 5, 1. Fred William Little.
        2. George Reed Little.
1, 4, 6, 8. Sarah A. Hayes, Canandaigua, N. Y.
1, 4, 6, 8, 1. Joseph Byron Hayes, M. D., Canandaigua, N. Y.
1, 4, 6, 8, 1, 1. Edward Graham Hayes, Canandaigua, N.Y.
        2. George Byron, Canandaigua, N. Y.
        3. Chester Coleman, Canandaigua, N. Y.
1, 4, 6, 2, 1. Charles Hammond Antes, New York City.
1, 4, 6, 2, 1, 1. William Sutherland Antes, New York City.
        2. May Ellis Antes, New York City.
        3. Alice Lee Antes, New York City.
1, 4, 6, 2, 3. Henry Taylor Antes, Genesee, Ill.

1, 4, 6, 2, 3, 1.	Helen Jeannette Antes, Genesee, Ill.
2.	Katharine Coleman Antes, Genesee, Ill.
1, 4, 6, 2, 4.	Robert Hayes Antes (twin with H. T. Antes.)
1, 4, 6, 7, 2, 1.	Bessie Barlow Reed, Weathersfield, Ill.
2.	Florence Bradley Reed, Weathersfield.
1, 4, 6, 7. 4, 2.	Frank M. Reed, Weathersfield, Ill.
	William Gardner, New York City.

5. Elizabeth, born January 29th, 1734. Her first husband was George Philip Dotterer of Frederick. The descendents of this marriage are known by the name of Dukehart, Sultzer, Blair, Wichelhausen, McCrea, Branson, and others. Among the descendents of these are several engineers. Her second husband was Rev. Nicholas Pomp, and their son Thomas Pomp was for fifty years pastor of the German Reformed Church, in Easton, Pa. Rev. Thomas Pomp had ten children, one of whom married Rev. Joseph F. Berg, D. D. Another one married Rev. Joseph B. Gross. Two are living.

1, 5, 7, 4.	Sophia Pomp, Easton, Pa.
1, 5, 7, 6.	Mary Catharine Pomp.
1, 5, 7, 2, 2.	His daughter Elizabeth married **Samuel** Kinsey.
1, 5, 7, 2, 1.	Thomas P. Kinsey, Reading, Pa.
1, 5, 7, 2, 1, 1.	Erwin P. Kinsey.
2.	Frank P. Kinsey.
3.	Ida Florence Kinsey.
4.	Walter Kinsey.
5.	Harry P. Kinsey.

1, 5, 7, 2, 1, 6. Samuel P. Kinsey.
1, 5, 7, 2, 1, 4, 1. Son.
              2. Daughter.
1, 5, 7, 2, 2, 1. Mary Black Kinsey.
           2. James Black Kinsey.
           3. Howard P. Kinsey.
1, 5, 7, 2, 3. Cornelia S. Stoneback, Easton, Pa.
1, 5, 7, 2, 3, 2. Henry B. Stoneback.
           3. Samuel Kinsey Stoneback.
           4. George Pomp Stoneback.
1, 5, 7, 2, 3, 3, 1. Cora Matilda Stoneback.
              2. Mary A. Haas.
1, 5, 7, 2, 5. Mary C. Green, Philadelphia, Pa.
1, 5, 7, 2, 5, 3. May Maxwell Green.
1, 5, 7, 2, 5, 3, 1. Margurite Green.
              2. Willie Green.
1, 5, 7, 2, 5, 5. Bessie S. Green.
1, 5, 7, 2, 6. George W. Kinsey, Lake Clear, Dakota.
1, 5, 7, 2, 6, 1. Daniel D. Kinsey.
           2. Edward Ingham Kinsey.
1, 5, 7, 2, 7. Amelia P. Green.
1, 5, 7, 2, 7, 3. Samuel Kinsey Green.
           4. Helen Thomas Green.
1, 5, 7, 2, 4. Samuel A. Kinsey.
1, 5, 7, 2, 4, 1. William E. Kinsey, Peoria Ill.
           2. Warren Kinsey.
           3. Nellie Kinsey.
           4. Blanche Kinsey.
           5. Ada Kinsey.
           6. Samuel Kinsey.
           9. Sarah E. Roberts, Wilkesbarre, Pa.
1, 5, 7, 2, 9, 1. Walter Owen Roberts.

1, 5, 7, 2, 10.   Emma Wilhelmina Berg, North Branch, N. J.
1, 5, 7, 2, 10, 1. Mary O. Berg.
           2. Sue P. Berg.
           3. Cassie Berg.
           4. Lizzie Berg.
           5. Minnie Berg.
           6. Grace Berg.
           7. Joseph F. Berg.
           8. Eva Berg.
           9. Ruth Berg.
1, 5, 7, 2, 11.   William Kinsey.
1, 5, 7, 9.   Elenora Pomp Berg.
1, 5, 7, 9, 1.   Mary Ellen Berg, Philadelphia.
           2. Anna Francis Berg.
           3. Joseph Frederick Berg.
           4. Amelia Pomp Berg.
           5. Herman Casper Berg.
           6. Elenora Berg.
           7. Sue Blanche Berg.
           8. Ida Thomas Berg.
           9. Kate DeWitt Berg.
1, 5, 7, 7.   Frederick W. H. Pomp.
1, 5, 7, 7, 1.   Thomas Herman Pomp.
           2. Anna Mary Pomp.
           3. William Henry Pomp.
           4. Emma Young Pomp.
           5. Julia Pomp.
1, 5, 7, 1, 2.   Charles Pomp.
1, 5, 7, 1, 2, 1. Belle Pomp Lawall, Easton, Pa.
           2. Sarah Pomp.
           3. Sue Pomp Maxwell.

4.	Mary K. Pomp.
5.	Emilie M. Pomp.
1, 5, 7, 10, 1.	Anna Pomp.

6. John Henry Antes, born October 5th, 1736. Was married twice. In 1775 he removed to Northumberland Co., Pa., was elected Justice of the Peace, was an ardent patriot, and built Antes Fort, at the junction of Antes creek with the Susquehanna, built a flouring mill under the protection of the fort, was Colonel of Militia for fighting Indians, served as Indian scout, was twice Sheriff, Judge of Quarter Sessions, and at times Presiding Judge.

1, 6, 1, 2, 1, 1.	Howard R. Antes (Rev.), Newark, Ill.
2.	Rebecca Minerva, Antes, Wheaton, Ill.
3.	Samuel Franklin Antes.
4.	Mary A. Antes.
6.	Charles Jacob Antes.
7.	Kate E. Antes.
10.	Henry Clayton Antes.
1, 6, 1, 2, 2.	Jacob Antes, Evansville, Wis.
1, 6, 1, 2, 2, 1.	Joseph Antes.
2.	Eli Antes.
3.	William Antes.
4.	Robert B. Antes
1, 6, 1, 2, 4.	Oscar Antes.
1, 6, 1, 3, 2.	David D. Antes, Centreville, Mich.
1, 6, 1, 3, 2, 1.	John D. Antes, Kansas City, Kansas.
1, 6, 1, 3, 3.	Samuel G. Antes, Santi Clara, Cal.
1, 6, 1, 3, 3, 1.	Ada Antes.
2.	Rulie Antes.
3.	William Antes.

1, 6, 1, 3, 4, 1.	Charles G. Bennet, New York City.
1, 6, 1, 3, 5.	Mrs. Jane E. Bennet, Three Rivers, Mich.
1, 6, 1, 3, 5, 1.	Claudia Bennett.
1, 6, 1, 3, 6.	Priscilla B. Daniels, Emporia, Kan.
1, 6, 1, 3, 6, 1.	Lemuel Clark.
2.	Howard Daniels.
1, 6, 1, 3, 7.	Charles A. Bressett, Three Rivers, Mich.
8.	William L. M. Antes, Aberdeen, Miss.
1, 6, 1, 3, 8, 1.	Edwin Henry Antes.
1, 6, 1, 3, 10.	Susanna M. Metzgar, Centreville, Mich.
11.	Amelia L. Bressett, Three Rivers, Mich.
1, 6, 1, 4, 1.	George W. Youngman (Hon.), Williamsport, Pa.
3.	Henry Antes Youngman, Grand Junction, Iowa.
4.	Caroline McMinn, Philadelphia.
8.	Amelia Louisa Sheadle.
9.	Priscilla Reichenbach.
10.	Martha Youngman, Williamsport, Pa.
11.	Elmira L. Jordan.
12.	Josephine E. Canfield.
13.	William T. Youngman.
1, 6, 1, 4, 1, 1.	Alonzo P. Youngman.
2.	Samuel L. Youngman, Williamsport, Pa.
3.	Geo. W. Youngman, Jr., Antes Fort, Pa.
4.	William L. Youngman.
5.	James M. Youngman, Williamsport, Pa.
6.	Mary L. Mehaffey.
8.	Charles W. Youngman (M. D).
1, 6, 1, 4, 4, 1.	Joseph H. McMinn, Williamsport, Pa.
2.	Charles V. L. McMinn, Newberry, Pa.
3.	Herman S. W. McMinn, Brooklyn, N. Y.

	4. Edwin McMinn (Rev.), Moorestown, N. J.
	5. Mary A. Grier, Newberry, Pa.
	6. Caroline Mackey, Philadelphia, Pa.
	7. Benjamin Franklin McMinn. Phila., Pa.
1, 6, 1, 4, 3,	1. Elias Youngman (has three children).
	2. Joseph Youngman.
	3. Mary Youngman Austin (has one child).
	8. Letitia Youngman Mecum.
1, 6, 1, 4, 5, 7.	Ada S. Youngman, Chicago, Ill.
1, 6, 1, 4, 7, 3.	Mrs. Florence Norris, Baltimore, Md.
	4. Mrs. Anna E. Archer, Dacotah.
1, 6, 1, 4, 8.	Mrs. Louisa Sheadle, Rochelle, Ill.
1, 6, 1, 4, 8, 1.	Miss Priscilla T. Sheadle.
	2. Miss Mary R. Sheadle.
1, 6, 1, 4, 9.	Mrs. Priscilla Reiderbach.
1, 6, 1, 4, 1, 2.	Mrs. Elmira Jordan, Necedah, Wis.
1, 6, 1, 4, 1, 3.	Josephine E. Canfield.
1, 6, 1, 4, 5, 1.	Stephen W. Youngman.
	3. Nancy E. Bushnell, Chicago, Ill.
	4. Stewart Youngman, Colorado.
	5. John Henry Youngman.
	6. Chas. B. Youngman, has four children.
	7. Ada S. Youngman, has two children.
1, 6, 1, 4, 7, 1.	Anna Elmira Archer, has six children.
	2. Florence Viola Roberts.
1, 6, 1, 4, 8, 1.	Priscil Viola Sheadle.
	2. Mary Rilla Sheadle.
1, 6, 1, 4, 1, 1, 1.	Steele T. Jordan.
	2. Josephene Jordan.
1, 6, 1, 4, 1, 2, 1.	Ella Antes Canfield.
	3. Clarence Canfield.

      4. Mattie Canfield.
      5. Harry Canfield.
      6. Baley Canfield.
1, 6, 1, 4, 1, 1, 1. Hattie Youngman.
      2. Anna Youngman.
1, 6, 1, 4, 1, 2, 1. William Sterling Youngman.
      2. Mary Youngman.
      3. Julia Ross Youngman.
1, 6, 1, 4, 1, 3, 1. May Youngman.
      2. Reynolds Youngman.
      3. Gardner Youngman.
      4. Ralph Youngman.
      5. Phœbe Youngman.
1, 6, 1, 4, 1, 4, 1. Walter Youngman.
      2. Emily Youngman.
1, 6, 1, 4, 1, 5, 1. Florence Youngman.
1, 6, 1, 4, 4, 1, 3. Caroline McMinn.
      4. David Ellis McMinn.
      5. Robert McMinn.
1, 6, 1, 4, 4, 2, 2. Charles Clayton McMinn.
      3. Herman McMinn.
1, 6, 1, 4, 4, 4, 2. George Rupert McMinn.
1, 6, 1, 4, 4, 5, 1. Emily Louisa Grier.
1, 6, 1, 4, 4, 6, 1. Stanley Mackey.
1, 6, 1, 5, 1. George Ruhl, Rockford, Ill.
    2. David Ruhl.
1, 6, 1, 9, 1. Mrs. Anna E. Foster, Elmira, N. Y.
    3. Henry Antes McMicken, Aberdeen Wis.
    4. Mrs. Irene J. Hamilton, Newark, N. J.
    5. Mrs. Margaret Huber, Williamsport Pa.
1, 6, 1, 8, 1. Antes Aughenbaugh, Antes Fort, Pa.
    2. Henrietta A. Bardo, Jersey Shore, Pa.

3.	Priscilla Aughenbach Barner, Antes Fort, Pa.
4.	George A. Aughenbaugh, Antes Fort, Penna.
6.	Daniel L. Aughenbaugh, Jersey Shore, Penna.
1, 6, 1, 8, 1, 1.	Francis C. Marcus, Antes Fort, Pa.
1, 6, 1, 8, 2, 1.	Jacob Bardo, Jersey Shore, Pa.
1, 6, 3, 1, 3.	Philip Antes, Nisbet, Lycoming Co. Pa.
1, 6, 3, 1, 3, 2.	Frederick T. Antes.
4.	Mrs. Mary K. Schaub.
6.	Horace P. Antes.
7.	Ira C. Antes.
1, 6, 3, 1, 4, 3.	Wm. C. Hollahan, Renova, Clinton Co., Penna.
4.	Thos. B. Hollahan, Lancaster, Lancaster Co., Penna.
5.	Mrs. Ettie McCormick, Lock Haven, Clinton Co., Penna.
6.	Miss Cora Hollahan.
1, 6, 3, 1, 5, 1.	Mrs. Elmira Campbell.
2.	Mrs. Dorcia Zimmerman.
3.	Mrs. Arabella Zimmerman.
4.	Mrs. Henrietta Thomas.
1, 6, 3, 1, 7.	Wm. W. Antes.
1, 6, 3, 1, 7, 2.	Mrs. Sarah Probst, Farrandsville, Clinton Co., Penna.
3.	Miss Mary Antes.
4.	William Antes.
5.	Andrew Antes.
1, 6, 3, 1, 9.	Mrs. Jane (Antes) Holter, Milesburg, Center Co., Penna.

1, 6, 3, 1, 9, 1. Joseph Holter.
2. Mrs. Constance, Phillipsburg, Center Co., Penna.
3. George Holter, Milesburg, Center Co., Penna.
4. Susan Holter, Milesburg, Center Co., Penna.
5. Mrs. Belle Van Scoy, Tyrone, Blair Co., Penna.
6. Mrs. Jennie Curtin, Roland, Center Co., Penna.
7. Mrs. Thanzene Walker, Phillipsburg, Center Co., Penna.

1, 6, 3, 1, 10, 1. Mrs. Martha J. Williams, Lock Haven, Clinton Co., Pa.
1, 6, 3, 2, 1. William Antes, Clearfield, Pa.
1, 6, 3, 2, 2. Mrs. Maria Stone.
3. James Antes.
4. Mrs. Elizabeth Fulton.
5. Mrs. Susan Irvin, Clearfield, Clearfield Co., Penna.
1, 6, 3, 3, 1. Mary Elizabeth Antes, Harrisburg, Pa.
4. John F. Antes.
5. Henry S. Antes.
6. J. Emory Antes.
1, 6, 3, 4. Gideon Goodfellow, Clearfield, Clearfield Co., Penna.
 Charles Rich, Lewistown, Mifflin Co., Pa.
1, 6, 3, 6, 1. John (Patton) Irwin, Curwinsville.
2. Mrs. Nancy (Patton) Beck, Pittsburg, Pa.
4. Mrs. Maria (Patton) Hipple.
5. Elizabeth Patton, Burnside township.

6.	John Patton, Curwinsville.
8.	Henry Patton.
1, 6, 3, 8.	Philip Antes.
1, 6, 3, 8, 1.	Lumsden Antes, Riverton.
2.	Alexander Antes.
3.	Mrs. Susan Antes Mitchell, Clearfield Co., Pa.
5.	Mrs. Elizabeth Antes, Riverton or Riverside, Clearfield Co., Pa.
1, 6, 3, 1, 1, 1.	Antes Canfield, Necedah, Wis.
3.	Thos. M. G. Canfield, husband of 1, 1,-6, 1, 4, 13, Josephine Youngman.
4.	Ira Canfield, Renova, Clinton Co., Pa.
5.	Mrs. Harriet Jane (Canfield) Christy.
6.	Mrs. Susan (Canfield) Straw, Texas.
8.	Mrs. Phœbe C. Canfield, Renova, Clinton Co., Pa.
	Horatio C. Crane, Lewistown, Idaho.
	Michael Albert Crane, Virginia City, Nevada.
1, 6, 4, 1, 1.	Henry Barnhart, Lockport, Ill.
2.	John Barnhart, Center Co., Pa.
3.	Philip Barnhart, Bellefonte.
4.	Smith Barnhart (Lawyer) Lockport, Ill.
5.	Mrs. Sarah Barnhart, Bellefonte, Center Co., Penna.
6.	Miss Elizabeth Barnhart.
1, 6, 4, 2, 1.	Philip W. Barnhart, Roland, Center Co.
2.	Henry L. Barnhart.
3.	Mrs. Julia Ann Curtin, her husband, John C., half brother to ex-Gov. Curtin.

	4.	Mrs. Sarah Sellers, Bellefonte, Pa.
	6.	Mrs. Nancy Kimport, Cherry Tree, Clearfield Co., Pa.
	7.	Mrs. Mary Davis, Hollidaysburg, Blair Co., Penna.
	8.	Mrs. Catharine Kimport.
1, 6, 4, 3.		Dr. John M. Barnhart, Vineland, Cumberland Co., N. J.
	2.	Hannah, widow of Rev. Thomas Coburg, Montgomery Co., Iowa.
	4.	Philip Barnhart, West Union, Fayette Co., Iowa.
1, 6, 4, 4.		Mrs. Elizabeth Barnhart, Barthrust.
	5.	John Barnhart.
	6.	Mary Barnhart, married James McChee.
	7.	Mrs. Ann Barnhart Ross, wife of John Ross, Curwinsville, Clearfield Co. Pa.
	8.	Mrs. Sophia Barnhart Johnson, one son, George Johnson, lives at Mt. Union Center Co., Pa.
	9.	Sarah Barnhart, twice married.
	10.	Christiana Barnhart Dopp. Mt. Eagle.
	11.	Catharine Barnhart Neff, Burnside Twp. Clearfield Co.
1, 6, 4, 2, 1, 1,		Mrs. Isabella Barnhart Oris, wife of Henry Oris, Milesburg, Centre Co., Pa.
	5.	Julia Barnhart Harshburger, P. O. Zion, Centre Co., Pa.
	6.	Joseph Barnhart, Renova, Clinton Co.
	7.	Mrs. Laura Barnhart Weaver, Bellefonte Centre Co., Pa.
1, 6, 4, 3, 1.		John M. Barnhart.

(Sister-in-law Hannah Coburg, Montgomery Co., Iowa.)
(Philip Barnhart, West Union, Fayette Co., Iowa.)

1, 6, 4, 3, 1, 1. C. K. Barnhart, Bolton's Block, Trenton, N. J.
         2. F. H. Barnhart, Washington, D. C.
         3. Elizabeth Ann Dougherty, Seymour, Webster Co., Mo.
         4. Mollie B. Kennedy, 820 Dekalb Ave., Brooklyn.
         5. Drusilla B. Messick, Vineland, N. J.
         6. Martin Ellsworth.

1, 6, 4, 2, 1, 3. Mrs. Lucy Barnhart, Roland Center Co., Pa.
         4. Amanda Barnhart.
         8. Henry Barnhart.
         9. Letitia Barnhart.
         10. James Barnhart.

1, 6, 4, 2, 2, 1. Alphonso Barnhart.
         2. John Barnhart.
         3. William Barnhart.

1, 6, 4, 2, 3, 1. James B. Curtin, Roland Center Co., Pa.
         2. Henry Curtin.
         3. John Curtin, Philadelphia, Pa.
         4. Mrs. Marjory Bell Curtin, Bellefonte, Ba.
         5. Mrs. Sarah (Curtin) Latimer.

1, 6, 7, 1, 2. Abel Dougherty.

1, 6, 1, 2, 2. Henry S. Antes, Jersey Shore, Lycoming Co., Pa.

1, 6, 12, 2, 1. James Antes, Elmira, N. Y.
         2. Miss Catherine A. Antes, Jersey Shore, Lycoming Co., Pa.

3.	Mrs. Mary F. Antes Caswell, Antes, Fort, Lycoming Co., Pa.
1, 6, 12, 3.	Mrs. Catharine (Antes) Messimer, Jersey Shore, Lycoming Co., Pa.
1, 6, 12, 3, 1.	Miss Emma Messimer, Jersey Shore.
2.	Miss Sarah E. Messimer.
3.	Joseph W. Messimer.
1, 6, 12, 4.	Mrs. Hannah (Antes) Leathers, wife of Jacob L., Roland Center Co., Pa.
1, 6, 12, 6.	Joseph Antes (deceased),—wife (living), Mrs. Martha K. Antes, Jersey Shore.

7. Jacob, born September 19th, 1738, died June 6th, 1739.

8. John, born March 13th, 1740. He became a missionary in Africa, a great traveler and an author. His work on Egypt, a quarto, attracted great attention at the time it was published. He also wrote several other works. He had no children.

9. Mary Magdalene, born October 28th, 1742. She went to Germany, was there married to Ebbing, died at Herrnhut, April 17th, 1811 and was buried in the Moravian Gottes Acker.

10. Joseph, born January 8th, 1745, died August 1746.

11. Benigna, born September 16th, 1748, died and was buried at Bethlehem in December, 1760.

Henry S. Doterer says in closing an account of Henry Antes, before the Deutscher Pionier Verein, April 28th, 1882, in the German Society Hall of Philadelphia: "The history of the Antes family shows that its membership is composed of an unusual large proportion of men of usefulness, ability and prominence. Henry Antes, the founder of the American branch, was a type of that hardy German element which came to Pennsylvania, settled on its inland frontiers, and stood a wall of protection between the treacherous savages and the favored dwellers in the towns. These people brought with them willing hands, untiring energy, and a steadfast faith in God. These characteristics have been transmitted through their posterity down to our times; and though, by reason of the changes wrought by time in their language, manners and names, we often fail to trace clearly the lineage of their succession, yet are the high principles of the forefathers still active, as they have been from the beginning, in moulding the morals and strengthening the bulwarks of the State. The Antes name we find, in the successive generations, ever in the van of enterprise. They are a race of builders; mechanics is their birthright. As we look upon the long line of honorable names we find many of them to excel as mechanics, engineers, architects, inventors and manufacturers. And when they turn from these pursuits to bear arms, to engage in the legal profession, or to assume the sacred office, the talent as workers in wood and metals, as has been shown, is still conspicuously present. When we contemplate the great numbers of the descendants of the pious layman of Frederick Township, scattered broadcast over the globe, the thoughts turn instinctively to the promise made to the patriarch of old: 'I will make thee exceedingly fruitful, and I will make nations of thee, and kings shall come out of thee.'"

SOCIAL & HISTORICAL STORIES

—BY—

REV. EDWIN MCMINN.

The Breaker Boy of Lansford.

A Story of the Coal Mines.
16mo, pp. 388.   Price, $1.25.

"Life in the mining regions is but little understood by those living in our large cities. The life is in general a rough one, but we have great respect for those stalwart sons of toil. The present volume gives an insight into their habits of life, their struggles, temptations, triumphs, and many interesting ways. We see, too, the softening and elevating power of the gospel, and that beneath a grimy exterior live noble souls who honor the Christian name and calling. There is an interesting sketch of the "Mollie Maguires." A large portion of the story is located at the Barclay Mines near the Wyoming Valley in this State, and at the Empire Mine near Wilkes Barre; while we find the whole mining region at the call and command of the author. Only a person thoroughly conversant with the topography of Pennsylvania, and with the life described could write such a book. We can highly commend it for its knowledge of the subject, its graphic descriptions, its intensely religious tone, and its rare adaption of the subject to a high purpose. It is sure to prove a most successful book for libraries in our Bible-schools, where wide-awake, yet thoroughly good books are in demand."—*National Baptist, Phila.*

Eaglesmere Trio.

A Temperance Story.
16mo. pp. 255.   Price, $1.00.

"The work depicts the career of three young men, who were thrown together when just approaching manhood. They were different in some important respects, but it was not easy to predict what their future career would be. The author traces them as they went along their pathway, in different scenes, meeting various influences, and notes their bearing in them.

As usual the temptations of the vender of ardent spirits had to be met; and also in the case of one, the evil influences of low politicians that are found in many localities working for evil. The tenors of their lives are well set forth and may readily be learned."—*Texas Baptist.*

Brave Hearts Win.
The Story of a Boot-Black.
12mo. pp. 255. Price $1.00.

" Brave Hearts Win is a book that boys will prize. It is the story of a lad stolen in his infancy from a Christian home of wealth and luxury, and brought up in neglect and poverty, but who won his way to education and position by 'clear grit' and faith in Christ. In his young manhood he discovers the secret of his birth and is restored to parents and home."—*Baptist Messenger.*

" There is also something of science presented in a pleasing way, &c.—*Arkansas Evangel.*

Judith and Glaucia.
A Story of the First Century.
16mo. pp. 407. Price, $1.50.

" There are thirty-seven chapters in this interesting story and eight full page pictures. Mr. McMinn has made much research as to the state of society in the time in which this scene is laid. The story begins before the martyrdom of Stephen, and carries us from Jerusalem to Antioch, Athens, Rome and Pella beyond the Jordan. It ends at the time of the fulfilment of prophecy in the memorable destruction of Jerusalem by the Roman forces under Titus. One of the heroines, Judith, was a Jewish maiden from Jerusalem and Glaucia was the daughter of a wealthy Athenian. Becoming acquainted they reach Antioch in the days when Paul was visiting it and preaching there. They were there brought to receive the gospel, and the course of their lives is traced until the narrative closes with the fall of Jerusalem."—*Christian Secretary, New Haven, Conn.*

Ben Ammi; The Armorer's Son.
A Story of the times of Isaiah.
12mo. pp 315. Price, $1.25.

" This work may be classed with 'The Prince of the House of David,' 'The Throne of David,' &c., as a historical novel. It rises above those mentioned, perhaps, in historical value. It compasses a particular and very interesting period in Israel's career, and depicts its character and events elaborately and with the constant use of the Bible narrative. We think it is well calculated not merely to entertain, but to assist the reader in Old Testament biography and ethics.—*Journal Messenger, Cinn., O.*

SOCIAL AND HISTORICAL STORIES.

The Bushkill Social.

The Boyhood of Fifty Boys Who became Celebrated Men. 12mo. pp.320. Price, $1.00.

"This is an admirable work for young folks, especially boys. It gives interesting sketches of noted persons. There is a thread of a story on which to string these bits of biography. There are poets, preachers, authors, presidents, sailors, explorers, &c. Evidently the Bushkill Social was an admirable society and we wish many such might be formed all over the country. The author is well known as a writer for young folks and we feel sure this will prove a popular work.—*Baltimore Baptist*.

All of the above published and for sale by the

American Baptist Publication Society,
1420 Chestnut St., Phila.

256 Washington St., Boston.   151 Wabash Ave., Chicago.
9 Murray St., New York.   1109 Olive St., St. Louis.

OTHER PUBLICATIONS BY THE SAME AUTHOR.

Rambles in Mineral Fields.

These are rambles in the mineral localities in Chester, Delaware and Lancaster counties, Pennsylvania, with full description of the scenery and minerals. Published in West Chester, Pa., 1878.

The Lycoming Rangers.

A story of a boys' retreat among the rocks of Lycoming Creek, in Pennsylvania, with discussions on educational and social questions. Published in Mahanoy City, 1881.

Pocket Manuel No. 3.

A compend of the choicest gleanings for the practical and the curious. Published in Philadelphia in 1884.

www.ingramcontent.com/pod-product-compliance
Lightning Source LLC
Chambersburg PA
CBHW022019240426
43667CB00042B/939